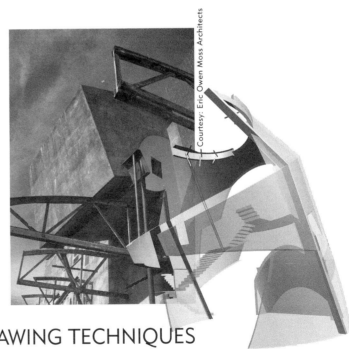

Courtesy: Eric Owen Moss Architects

HYBRID DRAWING TECHNIQUES
BY CONTEMPORARY ARCHITECTS AND DESIGNERS

Hybrid Drawing Techniques
by Contemporary Architects
and Designers

M. Saleh Uddin

John Wiley & Sons, Inc.

New York • Chichester • Weinheim • Brisbane • Singapore • Toronto

Stitching of photos and computer model · Courtesy: Eric Owen Moss Architects

Library of Congress Cataloging-in-Publication Data:

Uddin, M. Saleh (Mohammed Saleh)
     Hybrid drawing techniques by contemporary architects and designers
/ M. Saleh Uddin.
          p.   cm.
     ISBN 0-471-29274-5 (cloth : alk. paper)
     1. Composite drawing.   2. Architecture—Designs and plans—
Presentation drawings.   I. Title.
NA2714.U34   1999
720'.28'4—dc21   98-36474

This book is dedicated to the architects and illustrators who generously participated in this project and took their time to explain their drawings via phone, fax, e-mail, letter, and overnight mail.

Contents

Hybrids are the offspring of cross-fertilization between, more or less, distantly related parents. As a general rule, hybrids are intermediates between parental types in their morphological and physiological characteristics. Hybrids, in some cases, may become larger or more vigorous than either of their parents. This is true in all media, including visual ones. In terms of drawings and image manipulation, the combination of elements that are heterogenous in origin or composition will result in hybrids.

Plant and animal hybrids may arise spontaneously in nature or may be produced intentionally by man. A distinction, therefore, can be drawn between natural and artificial hybridization, but the characteristics of all hybrids are essentially the same. In all hybrids—whether in nature or manmade, in biological science or image communication—the elements or individuals that cross to produce them differ greatly in their genetic or hereditary makeup. The parental individuals may belong to different varieties, races, species, or even genera; the progeny derived from their crossing are known respectively as intervarietal, interracial, interspecific, or intergeneric hybrids.

The method of multimedia presentation itself is hybrid in its nature. Multimedia presentations derived from crossing image variations and diverse layers of sounds are much more vigorous and forceful than their individual parental layers. The same is true for static images when combined with other images with significant diversity.

Architects and designers have begun to experiment recently with multimedia presentation techniques for architectural drawings that reach beyond the purpose of mere presentation. As experimentation progressed, drawings evolved into the hybrid expression of several drawings combined into one, creating interest within the general population, as well as in the design community itself. In many instances, these new architectural drawings—composite drawings—have become valuable artifacts beyond their informational merit.

The scope of this book is to illustrate the strength of these composite graphics in design presentation. The book provides examples of composite hybrid drawings from contem-

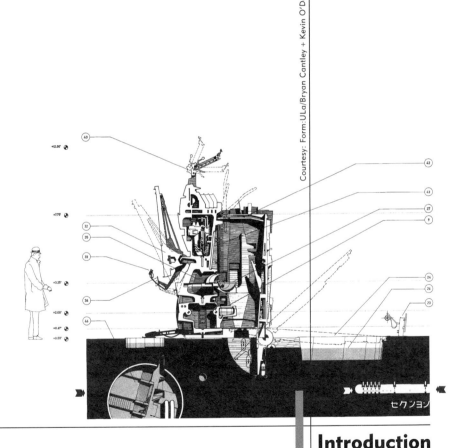

Courtesy: Form:ULa/Bryan Cantley + Kevin O'Donnell

Introduction

porary architects in Australia, Canada, Japan, Sweden, the United Kingdom, and the United States. It should be noted that the drawings in this book were drawn (in most cases) before the construction of a building, or in some cases for unrealized buildings. Such drawings often play an important role in the development of architectural ideas and new movements, and they are significantly different from drawings that merely present or document a building after it is finished.

Compared to the invention of still photography and its evolution into the motion picture, architectural drawing formats and conventions have lagged behind. Before the

advent of electronic technology, we did not see any new drawing types since the invention of perspective theory in the 15th century. The theory of axonometric drawing or parallel projection, another convention of three-dimensional drawing, also dates back to the time of the Italian Renaissance. If a new approach could be achieved that would bring together all known conventions (plan, elevation-section and three-dimensional views), architectural drawing would move into a new arena, in which the comprehensive overview of the design could be as important as its technological base.

If the intention of architectural drawings is to illustrate a total project or building, then logically, all architectural drawings should "read" as one drawing instead of a series of individual drawings representing segments of the building. When a composite drawing, illustrating sequential and integrated arrangement of individual drawings, is produced, the result is a dynamic and effective presentation of the total design. Composite drawings are particularly important in an academic environment, because students often present their drawings as individual pieces of information without prior thought about their arrangement or their relationship to each other. Requiring students to submit a design project as one composite drawing encourages planning the presentation beforehand and an increased comprehension of the total scope of the presentation.

The fusion of two or more drawings results in experimental hybrid graphics with variations in scale, type of drawing, reprographic technique, and the use of repetition and overlapping elements. Although combining a large number of diverse drawings into one drawing runs the risk of serious ambiguity (and could defeat the main purpose), com-

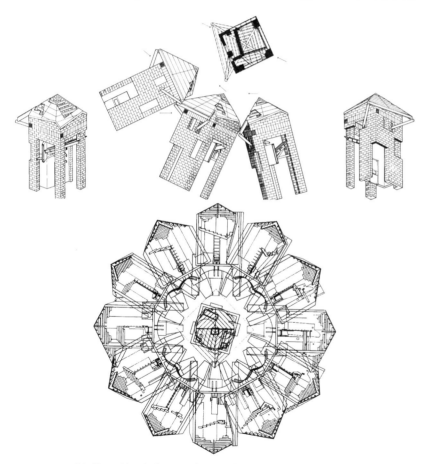

Eric Owen Moss's drawing showing plan, elevation, auxiliary, and oblique views (Lindblade Tower), and rotational section views (Indigent Pavilion).

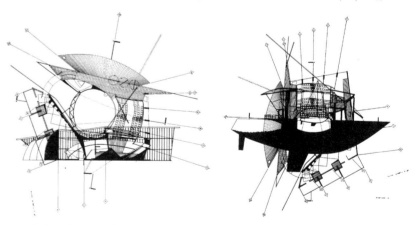

The logical fusion of plan and section drawings (during the design development process) results in experimental hybrid graphics, but may result in ambiguity (and could defeat the main purpose, if presented without the context of related drawings). Drawing by Joseph Dreher, Savannah College of Art and Design. M. Saleh Uddin, Studio Critic.

posite drawings offer opportunities to explore and experiment with the presentation, to emphasize, de-emphasize, compose and de-compose specific parts of a design drawing.

Hybrids are the fusion and superimposition of diverse drawing types intended to be seen as one drawing. Hybrids may be divided into three basic categories:

- Fusion and superimposition of ideas
- Fusion and superimposition of media
- Fusion and superimposition of techniques

Experimentation in all three categories is noticeable in recent student works at a number of architectural schools across the country.

Significant experimentation with layout is noticeable in recent architectural competition projects, in which each participant tries to arrange the maximum amount of information in a limited space. According to Tom Porter, "a major influence on this experimentation has been the growth of the international design competition and the subsequent publication of prize winners in design journals. As a result of the competition's restriction on size and the number of sheets, and the designer's need to catch the judge's eye in preliminary rounds of selection, this more dynamic and adventurous approach to layout design has evolved. The competition layout is characterized by considerable variation in the scale of drawings and the squeezing together, overlapping, and layering of graphic information within the format. Such layouts are carefully orchestrated, being

A wide variety of materials, including masonite board, corrugated brown board, plexiglass, gesso, metal screen sepia copy, acetate drawing and burnt drawings.
Drawing by Lee S. Mengt, University of Southwestern Louisiana.
George S. Loli and Dan Branch, Studio Critics.

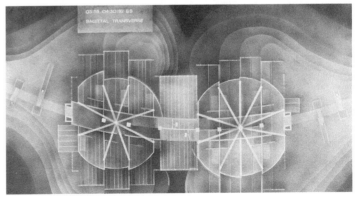

Breathing and characteristics of a tuberculosis cough are ideas integral to both project and representation. The chest activity and chest X-ray drawings were made with an atomizer by literally coughing ink through a tube onto the sheet. The final project drawings were all done with airbrush on Mylar (a coughing/breathing machine).
Drawing by J. C. Smith, University of Colorado. Douglas Darden, Studio Critic.

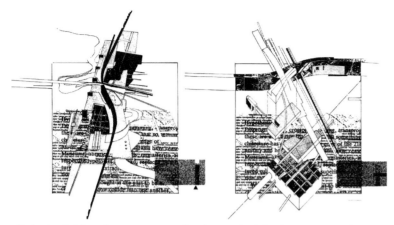

Text extracted from the program as well as key words of the design concept photocopied at various scales and intensities to create texture and grain in the drawing. Text surface capable of creating additional visual layer and informative layer. Drawing by Ron Yong + Sharlene Young, Ohio. "Urbanconnector" Linear City.

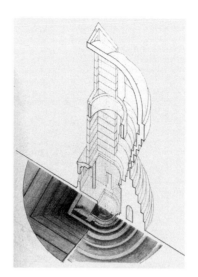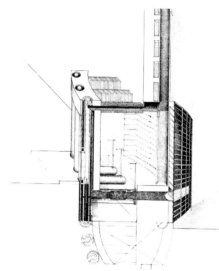

Synthesis drawing using all of the three basic projection types (orthographic, axonometric, and perspective) all constructed from one another as linked multiple views. Drawing by Bruce Brunner and Jason Landrum, University of Arkansas. Randall Ott, Studio Critic.

Monochrome sepia-like color drawing with Toblerone Swiss chocolate brings translucent quality against light source. See Color Plate 1. Drawing by George S. Loli, Associate Professor, University of Southwestern Louisiana.

reminiscent of how an artist might plan an abstract composition. Indeed, the assembly of a series of multiview fragments into the frozen dynamic of a large and complex layout has obvious roots in Cubism and Constructivism.

Even though modernism has patronized straightforward, informative, separate drawings, some architects have continued to place value on the pleasing presentation of their work. In many cases, the quality of the architectural drawing stood out only on those projects in which getting the building constructed was not a serious consideration. While breaking away from the pragmatist tradition of the 1950s, many new ideas became unveiled through visions for an architectural utopia. Archigram in England and the Metabolists in Japan and Vienna, for instance, suggested a complete, attainable environment in their drawings rather than representing the structure to be built.

In its departure from modernism, the postmodern period introduced new directions in architectural drawing. Aldo Rossi in Milan, Oswald Mathias Ungers in Berlin, Raimund Abraham and Rob Krier in Vienna, and Leon Krier in London all emphasized the relative independence of architectural drawings and led to a new aesthetic, which eventually became recognized in its own right. Among American architects, Charles Moore, Michael Graves, John Hejduk, Robert Venturi, Steven Holl, and Peter Eisenman are the pioneers. Most New Age architects did not conceive of drawings merely as documents

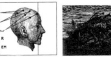

Dis/continuous Genealogies
Earth Mound
Dante's *Inferno* XVII, reversed Doré'
Monck's *Account of a Most Dangerous Voyage*
Polygraphic record of a patient
Composite Ideogram

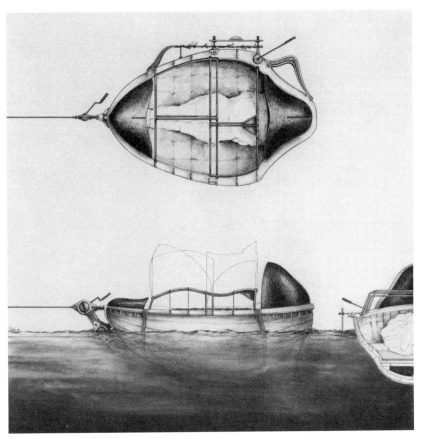

Douglas Darden's "Dis/continuous Genealogies" is a composite of iconography, structure, formal composition, and program of the architectural project, thereby developing the design from logic and findings.

KITCHEN · BREAKFAST · BALCONY

Richard B. Ferrier combined photography and hand-drawing to produce this hybrid composite "Photo-sketch for Douglas Lake House," a conceptual spatial presentation of on-site progress. See Color Plate 17.

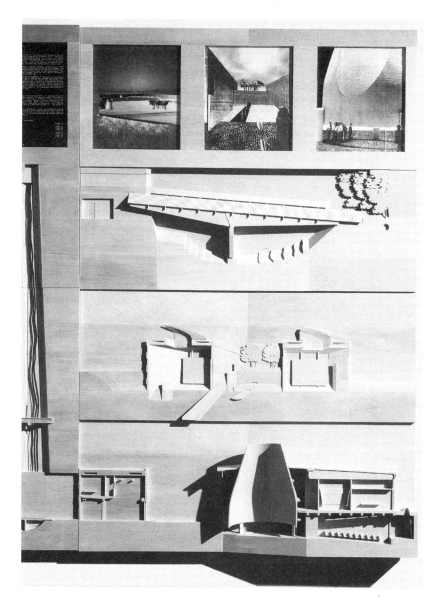

Todd Williams Billie Tsien's relief drawing in a basswood presentation combines model-making technique and drawing.

for construction. Rather, drawings were seen as a medium of expression for igniting a new agenda for architecture. In addition, the emphasis of drawings by Anthony Ames, Tadao Ando, Douglas Darden, Neil Denari, Richard Ferrier, Steven Holl, house+house, Frank Israel, Helmut Jahn, Morphosis, Eric Owen Moss, Peter Pran, Carlo Scarpa, Shin Takamatsu, and Bernard Tschumi, in many instances, seems to communicate information through an unconventional means of drawing interpretation.

Douglas Darden's "Dis/continuous Genealogies" for the project Clinic for Sleep Disorders represents a hybrid conceptualization of iconography, structure, formal composition, and program of the architectural project. This incorporates a process of developing design from logic and findings (figure).

Richard B. Ferrier's composite "Photo-sketch for Douglas Lake House" is a conceptual spatial presentation of on-site progress created by combining photographs and hand drawings (figure).

The proposal by Helmut Jahn for the St. Paul Convention Center and Hotel shows a new approach toward a three-dimensional composite graphic presentation. It is a collage of various types of drawings summarizing the concept of the design on a scroll, in the form of a reel on acrylic glass spools (figure). For Helmut Jahn, composite drawings are more like unfolding a model to reveal various concerns of a design in one drawing. In many of his drawings, rays and beams of light represent the energy and interaction of natural light within the building and the building light emanating outward from within.

For Eric Owen Moss, composite drawings are a manifestation and a record of changes and amendments made as the project evolves. The composite drawings are made to provide a comprehensive understanding of the buildings from start to finish, from all angles. While they have an intrinsic beauty in themselves, their main function is to inform thoroughly. The rotational section views for the Indigent Pavilion and the projected plan, elevation, auxiliary, and oblique views for Lindblade Tower create a full 360° rotational view, which would be impossible to show with conventional single-view drawings.

Bernard Tschumi's drawing for the Parc de la Villette in Paris (figure) shows effective superimposition of lines, points, and surfaces, emphasizing the layers of landscape and built elements.

A series of composite superimpositions of plan and elevation drawings by Morphosis for The Comprehensive Cancer Center in Los Angeles (figure) illustrates the rotation of the moving element at different angular orientation and exploration of the fourth dimension, time. This creates a visual image of movement inclining toward an animation effect. A series of section drawings, taken in a particular sequence by Morphosis for the Lawrence House, shows us a three-dimensional animated effect, suggesting the possibility of a strip of motion picture illusion.

The proposal by Helmut Jahn for the St. Paul Convention Center and Hotel is a collage of various types of drawings, which epitomize the design concept on a scroll consisting of a reel on acrylic glass spools.

A series of vertical layers of plans ("force planes") rendered in progressive luminosity and translucency by Zareen M. Rahman created in AutoCAD and 3D Studio Max intends to produce a lucid and cogent spatial analysis for an urban project. Through the mode of translucency, hidden patterns could thus emerge and be read in parallel within the existing site fabric.

A digital collage by Peter Pran, Jonathan Ward and Dan Mies of NBBJ for the interior of the Seoul Dome, Seoul, Korea, illustrates the hybrid nature of the enclosed environment (figure) through the exploration of the digital media. A series of diverse image types arranged on a post-card for the same project demonstrates the notion of providing multiple image information and readings in the format of a high-tech mini billboard.

The nature of hybrid drawings has changed our perception and expectations about the role of architectural drawing. Although a hybrid drawing communicates on many levels beyond utility, it is also perceived as an artwork, a prized artifact that endures beyond the completion of a project. The contemporary influence of composite hybrid graphics suggests that designers will learn a new method of reading and drawing the fourth dimension, acknowledging the nonstationary nature of architectural views.

These examples, as well as works featured by more than 50 architects and designers, speak to the significant changes occurring in architectural representation. The power and effectiveness of multilayered expression of graphics make this new form a presence too important to be ignored.

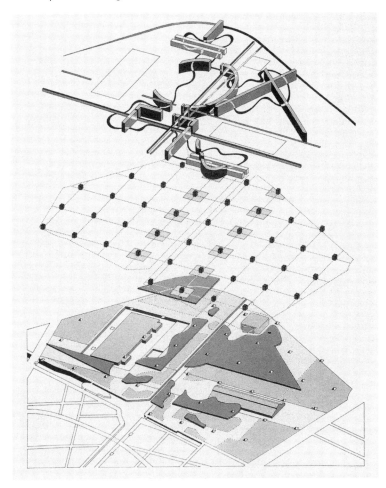

Bernard Tschumi's drawing for the Parc de la Villette in Paris, effectively superimposing lines, points, and surfaces, emphasizes the layers of landscape and constructed elements.

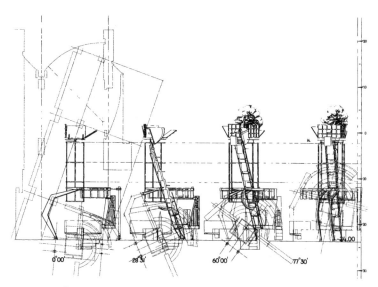

Composite superimpositions of plan and elevation drawings by Morphosis for The Comprehensive Cancer Center in Los Angeles demonstrates how the moving element rotates at different angular orientations and explores the fourth dimension, time.

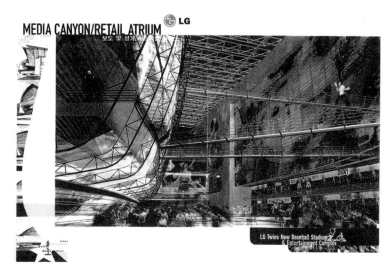

Digital collage by Peter Pran, Jonathan Ward, and Dan Mies of NBBJ Sports & Entertainment illustrates the hybrid nature of the interior environment for the Seoul Dome (LG Twins Baseball Stadium/2002 World Championship Football Stadium + Entertainment Center), Seoul, Korea.

Zareen M. Rahman layered a series of vertical plans ("force planes") in progressive luminosity and translucency to illustrate the perceptual study of site lines in an urban study. See Color Plate 50.

A series of diverse image types arranged on a post card by Peter Pran, Jonathan Ward, and Dan Mies of NBBJ Sports & Entertainment illustrates the notion of combining design excellence and digital technology in the format of a mini billboard. See Color Plate 2.

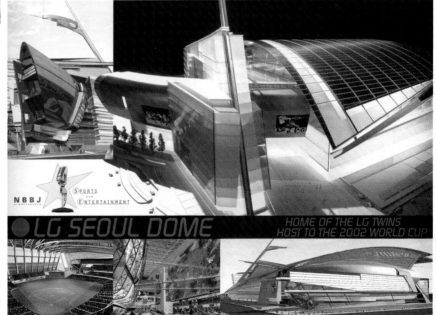

Plate 1. Monochrome sepia-like color drawing with Toblerone Swiss chocolate brings translucent quality against light source. Drawing by George S. Loli, Associate Professor, University of Southwestern Louisiana.

Plate 2. A series of diverse image types arranged on a post card by Peter Pran, Jonathan Ward, and Dan Mies of NBBJ Sports & Entertainment illustrates the notion of combining design excellence and digital technology in the format of a mini billboard.

Plate 3. House in Mississippi, Laurel, Mississippi.
Design and drawing: Anthony Ames Architect

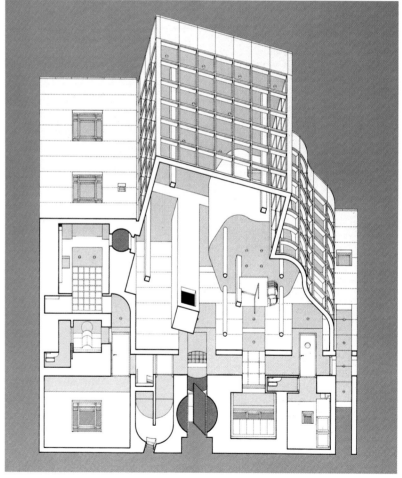

Plate 4. Martinelli Residence, Roxbury, Connecticut.
Design and drawing: Anthony Ames Architect

Plate 5. Sunshelter Project, New York, New York.
Design and drawing: Benjamin H. Ames

Plates 6 and 7. Sunshelter Project, New York, New York.
Design and drawing: Benjamin H. Ames

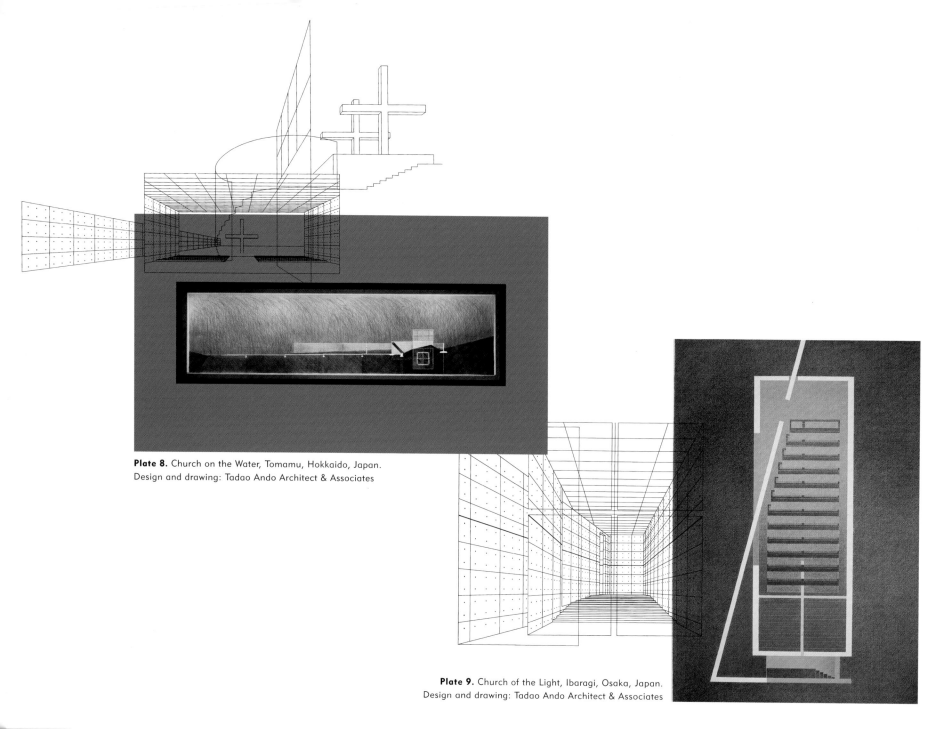

Plate 8. Church on the Water, Tomamu, Hokkaido, Japan.
Design and drawing: Tadao Ando Architect & Associates

Plate 9. Church of the Light, Ibaragi, Osaka, Japan.
Design and drawing: Tadao Ando Architect & Associates

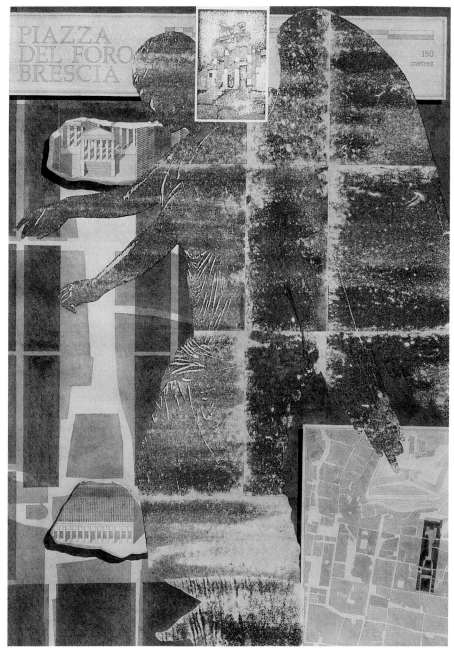

Plate 10. Piazza del Foro, Brescia, Italy.
Drawing: Eamonn Canniffe.

Plate 12. Sega World, Darling Harbor, Sydney, Australia.
Design: Daryl Jackson Architects, Australia
Drawing: Peter Edgeley, Australia

Plates 13 and 14. Piazza and Ferry Terminal
near Sydney Opera House, Sydney, Australia.
Design: Greg-Scott-Young/EMTB Architects, Australia
Drawing: Peter Edgeley, Australia

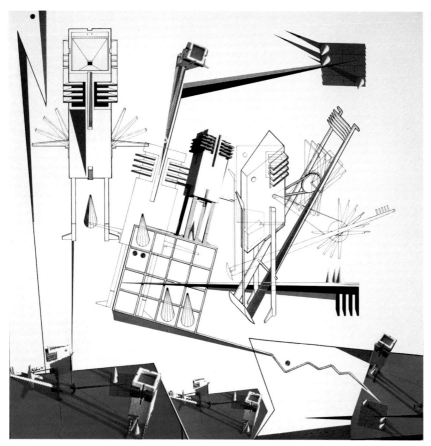

Plate 15. Anthromorphs.
Design and drawing: Robert J. Fakelmann

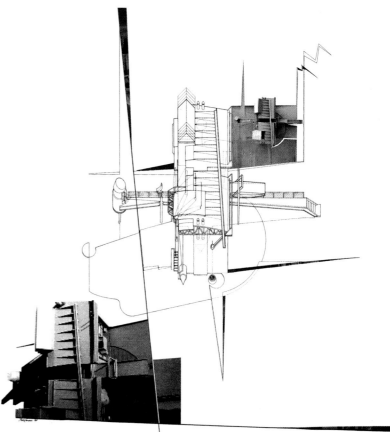

Plate 16. The His and Her House.
Design and drawing: Robert J. Fakelmann

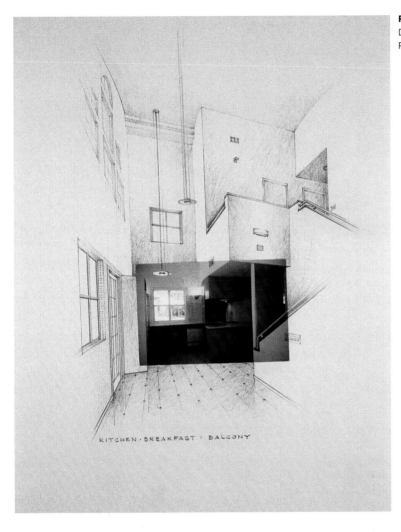

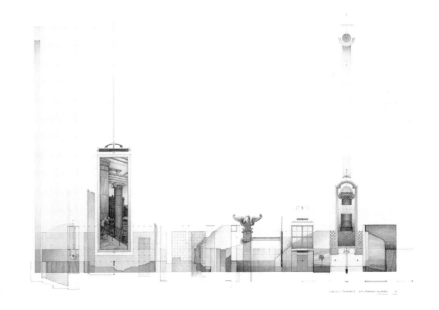

Plate 17. GBC Douglas Lake House, Lake Texamco, Texas.
Drawing: Richard B. Ferrier
Photographer: C. Kuhner

KITCHEN · BREAKFAST · BALCONY

Plate 18. Windows and Fragments: Karl Friedrich Schinkel.
Drawing: Richard B. Ferrier, FAIA

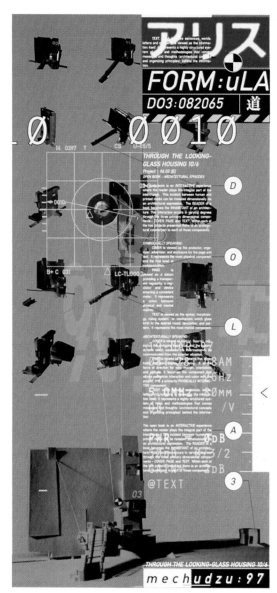

Plate 19. Through the Looking Glass Housing.
Design: Bryan Cantley + Kevin O'Donnell
Photos: Jan Bruins + Bryan Cantley

Plate 20. Outhouse Prototype [urban variant] No. 93.7, Poster No. 2.
Design and drawing: Bryan Cantley + Kevin O'Donnell

Plate 22. Philadelphia Commercial Project, Philadelphia.
Design: Dan Mies for Ellerbe Becket, Inc., Los Angeles
Rendering: Gilbert Gorski

Plate 23.
AARP Addition, Washington, DC.
Drawing: Harlan Hambright/InSite

InSite™

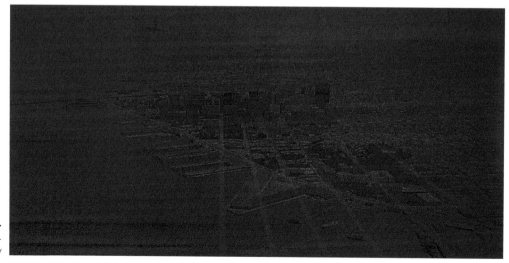

Plate 24.
San Francisco Waterfront Competition (SFO-001).
Design and drawing: Erik M. Hemingway

Plates 25 and 26. McGhee Tyson Airport, Knoxville, Tennessee.
Drawing: HNTB Architecture

Plate 27 (three images below). Langmaid Residence, Oakland, California.
Architects: house+house
Drawing: David Haun

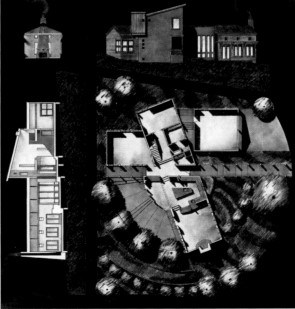

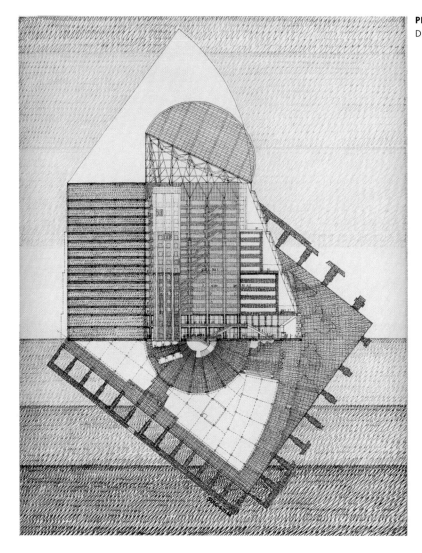

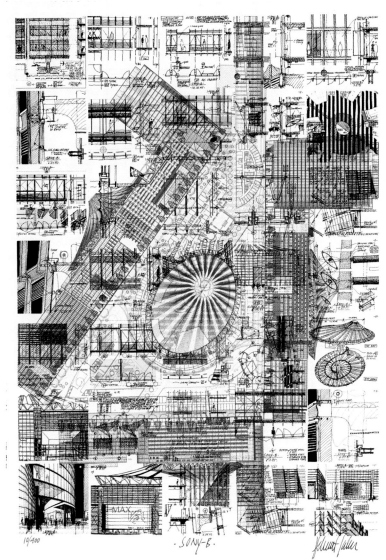

Plate 28. State of Illinois Center, Chicago, Illinois.
Drawing: Helmut Jahn

Plate 29. Sony Center Berlin, Berlin, Germany.
Drawing: Helmut Jahn

Plate 30. Northwestern Atrium Center, Chicago, Illinois.
Drawing: Helmut Jahn with T. J. McLeish

Plate 31. A Center for the Study of Television and Film (Academic Project).
Design, drawing, and photography: Keelan P. Kaiser

Plate 32 (four images above).
Claflin Work/Live Studios.
Design: Keelan P. Kaiser,
Thomas Gallagher
Drawing: Matt Stoffel
Photography: Keelan P. Kaiser

Plate 33. Office Building, Tokyo, Japan.
Design: A. Scott Howe and Tomohito Okudaira for Kajima Corporation
Rendering: A. Scott Howe

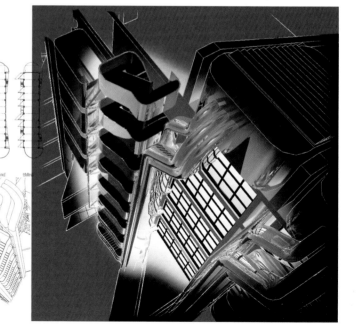

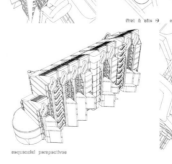

Plate 34. Memorial Hall Project, Kushiro, Japan.
Design: A. Scott Howe and Yuji Kaido for Kajima Corporation
Rendering: Chizuko Sami

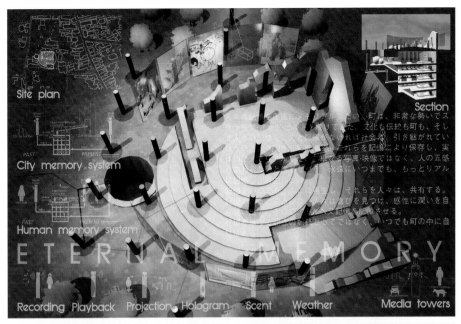

Plate 35. PAVILION project, Tokyo, Japan.
Architectural design: A. Scott Howe and Hiroshi Ono for Kajima Corporation
Rendering: Go Nishiyama

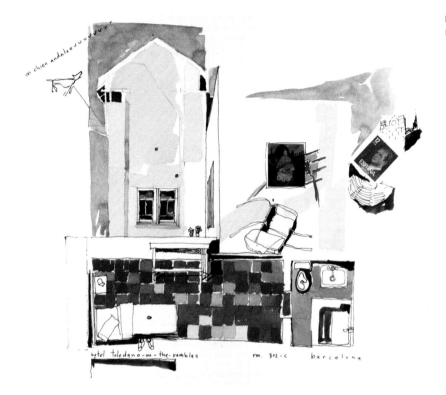

Plate 36. Room 302-C, Hotel Toledano-on-the-Ramblas, Barcelona.
Drawing: Peter Kommers

Plate 37. San Marco Orphanage, Siena, Italy.
Drawing: Elizabeth Grossman

Plate 38. Faktura—Earth.
Digital Drawing: Logic Error
Designers: Derek Robert McCallum, Glasgow School of Arts, Scotland
Chris Mullen, Sci-arc
David Eric Koenen, University of Minnesota
Joey Myers, North Dakota State University
Paul Quinn Davis, University of Minnesota
Michael Hnastchenko, University of Minnesota

Plate 39. Cylindrical House "Calderara," Emperia, Italy.
Drawing: George S. Loli

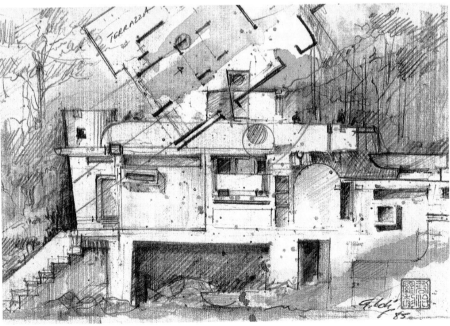

Plate 40. Villa a Scandicci, Florence, Italy.
Drawing: George S. Loli

Plates 41 and 42. O'Neill Guesthouse, Brentwood, California.
Design and drawing: Susan Lanier and Paul Lubowicki

Plate 43. Project for the Via della Conciliazione, Rome.
Drawing: David Thomas Mayernik

Plate 44. Arts Park Performing Arts Pavillion.
Design and drawing: Thom Mayne with Hans Boelling

Plate 45. Seventy-Two Market Street.
Design and drawing: Thom Mayne with Kazu Arai

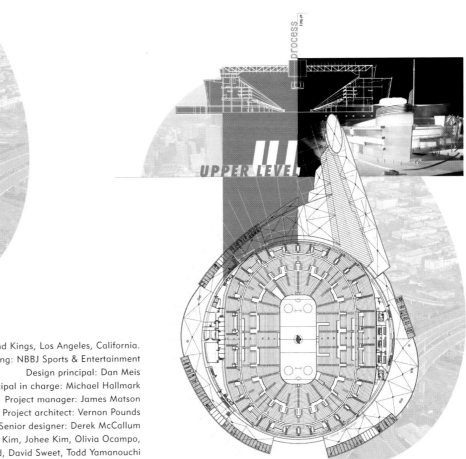

Plate 46. Staples Center—Home of the Los Angeles Lakers and Kings, Los Angeles, California.
Design and drawing: NBBJ Sports & Entertainment
Design principal: Dan Meis
Principal in charge: Michael Hallmark
Project manager: James Matson
Project architect: Vernon Pounds
Senior designer: Derek McCallum
Project team: Rania Alomar, Robert Dittes, Patrick Fejer, Fred Kim, Johee Kim, Olivia Ocampo, Heidi Painchaud, David Sweet, Todd Yamanouchi
Model and photography: John Lodge

Plate 47. Staples Center—Home of the Los Angeles Lakers and Kings, Los Angeles, California.
Design and drawing: NBBJ Sports & Entertainment
Design principal: Dan Meis
Principal in charge: Michael Hallmark
Project manager: James Matson
Project architect: Vernon Pounds
Senior designer: Derek McCallum
Project team: Rania Alomar, Robert Dittes, Patrick Fejer, Fred Kim, Johee Kim, Olivia Ocampo,
Heidi Painchaud, David Sweet, Todd Yamanouchi
Model and photography: John Lodge

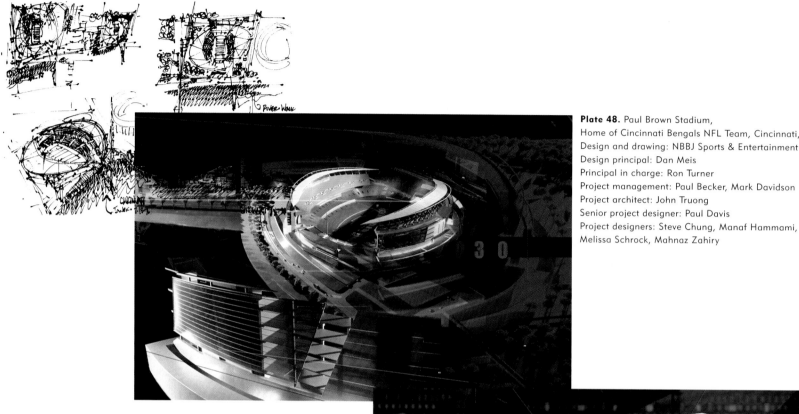

Plate 48. Paul Brown Stadium,
Home of Cincinnati Bengals NFL Team, Cincinnati, Ohio.
Design and drawing: NBBJ Sports & Entertainment
Design principal: Dan Meis
Principal in charge: Ron Turner
Project management: Paul Becker, Mark Davidson
Project architect: John Truong
Senior project designer: Paul Davis
Project designers: Steve Chung, Manaf Hammami,
Melissa Schrock, Mahnaz Zahiry

Plate 49. Paul Brown Stadium,
Home of Cincinnati Bengals NFL Team, Cincinnati, Ohio.
Design and drawing: NBBJ Sports & Entertainment
Design principal: Dan Meis
Principal in charge: Ron Turner
Project management: Paul Becker, Mark Davidson
Project architect: John Truong
Senior project designer: Paul Davis
Project designers: Steve Chung, Manaf Hammami,
Melissa Schrock, Mahnaz Zahiry

Plate 50. Space-Form Analysis Schematic.
Drawing: Zareen Mahfooz Rahman

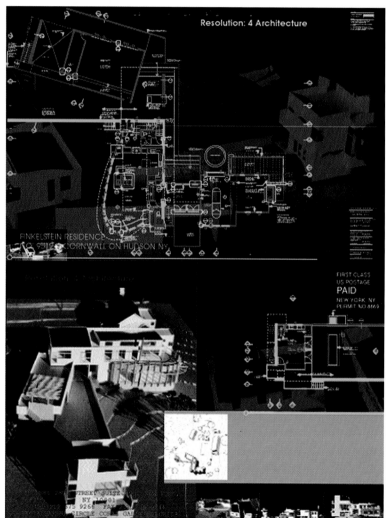

Plate 51. Hortus Poeticus, Beverly Hills, California.
Drawing: Thomas Norman Rajkovich

Plate 52. Finkelstein Residence, 9512 Cornwall on Hudson, New York.
Project architect: John DaCruz
Principals: Joseph Tanney, Robert Luntz
Project team: Heather Roberge, Clay Collier, Eric Liftin, Setu Shah,
Jennifer Pereira, Mario Gentile, Jeffrey Dvi-Vardhana, Kevin Bergin
Postcard: Setu Shah

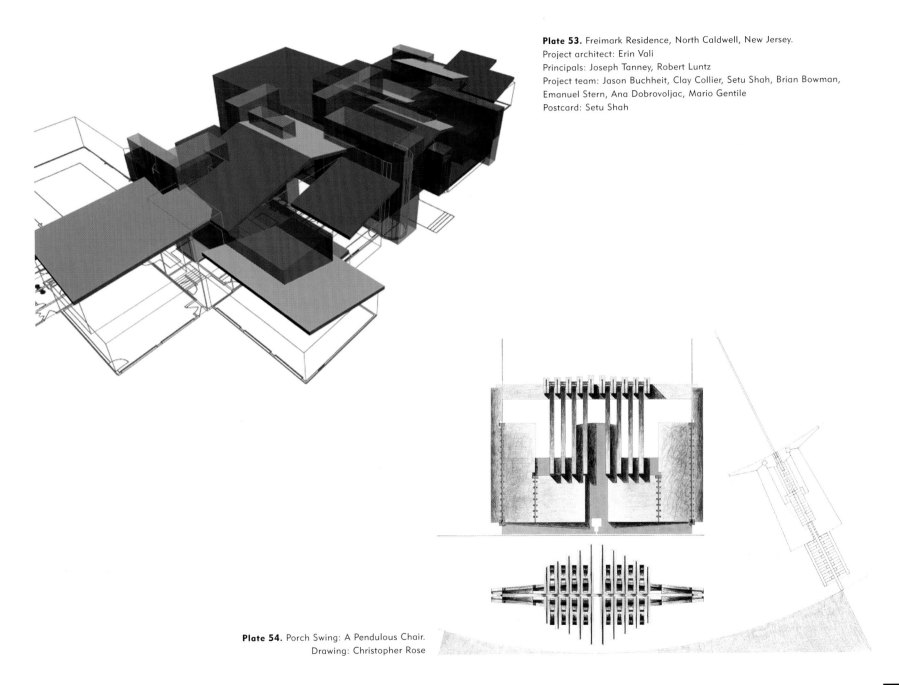

Plate 53. Freimark Residence, North Caldwell, New Jersey.
Project architect: Erin Vali
Principals: Joseph Tanney, Robert Luntz
Project team: Jason Buchheit, Clay Collier, Setu Shah, Brian Bowman,
Emanuel Stern, Ana Dobrovoljac, Mario Gentile
Postcard: Setu Shah

Plate 54. Porch Swing: A Pendulous Chair.
Drawing: Christopher Rose

NEW YORK NEWSSTAND

Plate 56. Wales Opera House Competition, Wales, United Kingdom.
Design: Ashton Smith and Dan Branch
Drawing: Ashton Smith

Plate 57. Shilla Daechi Building (as shown at the Venice Bienniale, 1996).
Design and drawing: Smith-Miller + Hawkinson Architects

Plate 58. Corning Glass Center 2000.
Design and drawing: Smith-Miller + Hawkinson Architects

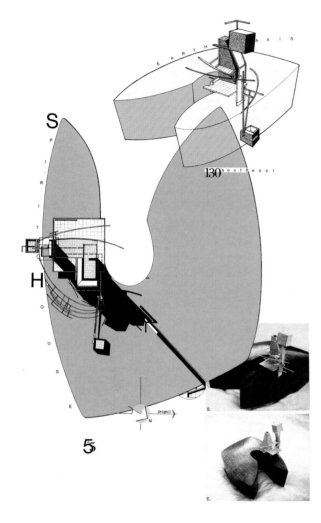

Plate 59. Spirit House 5.
Design and drawing: Thomas Sofranko

Plate 60. Kunibiki Messe, Matsue, Japan.
Design and drawing: Shin Takamatsu Architects & Associates

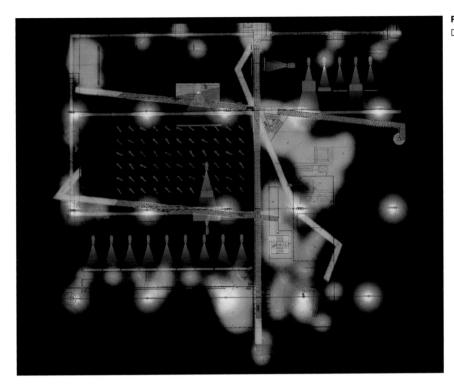

Plate 61. In Between, Le Fresnoy National Studio for Contemporary Arts, Tourcoing, France.
Design and drawing: Bernard Tschumi Architects

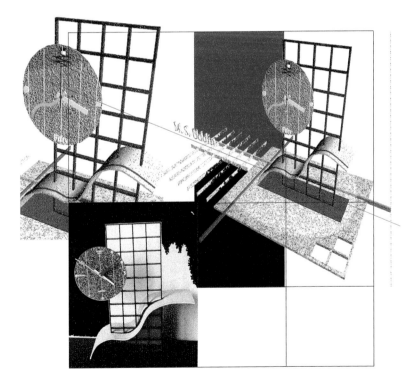

Plate 62. Grid Clock.
Design and drawing: M. Saleh Uddin

Plate 63. Rahman Residence, Dhaka, Bangladesh.
Design and drawing: M. Saleh Uddin

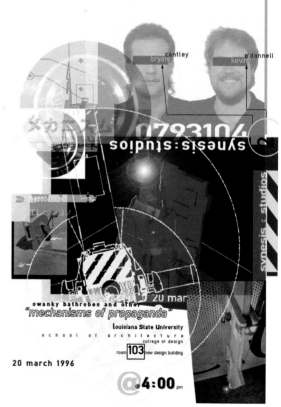

Plate 64. LSU Lecture Poster.
Courtesy: Form:uLA/Bryan Cantley + Kevin O'Donnell

• Takefumi Aida (Japan) • Anthony Ames Architect • Benjamin H. Ames • Tadao Ando (Japan) • R. L. Binder, FAIA, Architecture & Planning • Eamonn Canniffe (England) • Douglas Darden • John J. Desmond, FAIA • Peter Edgeley for Daryl Jackson Architects (Australia) • Robert Evans (England) • Robert J. Fakelmann • Richard B. Ferrier, FAIA • Form:uLA/Bryan Cantley + Kevin O'Donnell • Thomas P. Gallagher • Gilbert Gorski • Gordon Grice (Canada) • Harlan Hambright/Insite for Kohn Pederson Fox, Architects • Erik M. Hemingway • HNTB Architecture • house+house • the hut • Inglese Architecture • Helmut Jahn • Keelan P. Kaiser • Kajima Corporation (Japan) • Peter Kommers • Sandra Davis Lakeman (with Elizabeth Grossman) • Logic Error • George S. Loli • Lubowicki/Lanier Architects • William E. Massie • David Thomas Mayernik • Morphosis • Eric Owen Moss • NBBJ Sports & Entertainment • Alexis Pontvik Arkitekt (Sweden) • Zareen Mahfooz Rahman/ Studio-Z (England) • Thomas Norman Rajkovich • Resolution: 4 Architecture • Christopher Rose • Schwartz Architects • Jeffrey L. Sheppard of Roth + Sheppard Architects • Ashton Smith • Ashton Smith with Dan Branch • Smith-Miller + Hawkinson Architects • Thomas Sofranko • Shin Takamatsu (Japan) • Christine L. Tedesco • Bernard Tschumi Architects • M. Saleh Uddin • Mehrdad Yazdani • Art Zendarski for Dworsky Associates, Los Angeles • ████████████

Drawing: Form:uLA/Bryan Cantley + Kevin O'Donnell

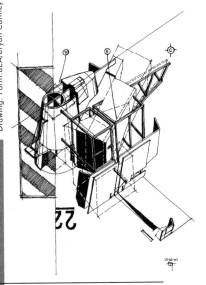

Hybrid Drawings

Takefumi Aida

Takefumi Aida Architect & Associates, Tokyo, Japan

Furuse House, Shimane Prefecture, Ohara, Japan

Profile

The work of Japanese architect Takefumi Aida spans cultures both East and West—from shoji screens to semiology, from Noh drama to deconstructivism. Aida's early work questions the modernist dictum that form follows function, rather than design sensibility. Using planes to layer site, space, activity, and symbol is one of the significant features of his work. Mr. Aida has received a number of prestigious design awards for his architectural work and has taught at Shibaura Institute of Technology in Tokyo for a number of years. He established his own firm, Takefumi Aida Architect & Associates, in 1967.

Explanation of the Drawing Process and Technique

Hand-drawn in ink on Japanese paper.

Purpose of the Drawing

The drawing expresses the concept of "Yuragi"—fluctuation and composition of spaces in the building with shading of each element of wall.

Design Concept

The architecture is composed of several parallel walls and posts, independent of functions created by them. There is no coherence between architectural elements and their functions. Between the relationship of these elements and each function, a chaotic space is created. An observer may see this chaotic space as an invisible space, a spatial effect of Yuragi—fluctuation.

Furuse House, Shimane Prefecture, Ohara, Japan.
Drawing: Takefumi Aida

Takefumi Aida

Takefumi Aida Architect & Associates, Tokyo, Japan

GKD Building, Hiroshima, Japan

Explanation of the Drawing Process and Technique

Hand-drawn with pencil on Japanese paper.

Purpose of the Drawing

Drawing shows the concept of "Yuragi"—fluctuation, and composition of spaces by layering of the walls.

Design Concept

The design intends to create a context different from the prevailing ambience, to suggest a new way in which the streetscape and the area in general could develop, and to provide the GKD Building with its own identity. In order to achieve this objective, multiple planar fragments, each endowed with a distinct image, are arranged in layers. This expresses the uneven and unstable process by which Japanese cities develop and provides an effective means of reinvigorating the area. Some planes are tilted and others are very orderly and independent. The shoji-like aluminum curtain wall and the huge aluminum lattice inserted among the planes are also distinct objects.

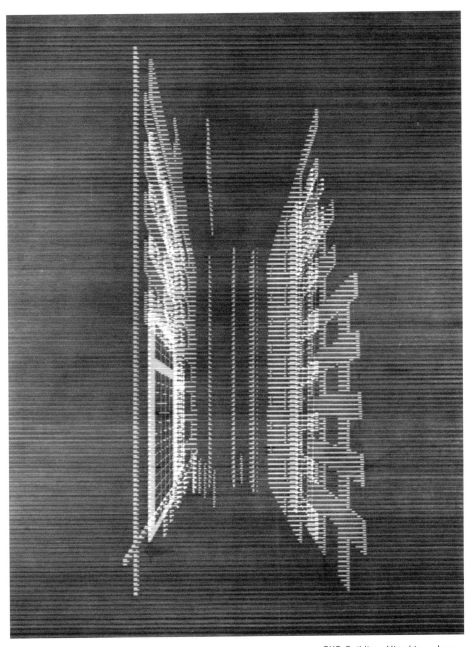

GKD Building, Hiroshima, Japan.
Drawing: Takefumi Aida

Atlanta, Georgia

House in Mississippi, Laurel, Mississippi

Profile

Anthony Ames received his architectural education from Harvard University and Georgia Tech and is a fellow of the American Academy of Rome. His work has received design awards from *Progressive Architecture* magazine, *Architectural Record* magazine, and the American Institute of Architects. He has taught architecture at Columbia University, the Rhode Island School of Design, Harvard University, Princeton University, Georgia Tech, the University of Virginia, and other schools. He currently maintains an office in Atlanta, Georgia, Anthony Ames Architect.

Explanation of the Drawing Process and Technique

Interior composed view. Color adhesive film on photographic print of ink line drawing.

Purpose of the Drawing

The drawing illustrates the entry sequence, in which the visitor is encouraged to look through the living space to the landscape beyond, but is denied access to this space by a built object and is forced to move perpendicular to the entry along the edge of the space.

Design Concept

Two rotated rectangles are superimposed in such a manner that the residual space created between the perimeters of each is treated as an occupiable poche and contains the vertical circulation (stairs) and the service facilities. Spaces are arranged in two diverse types, establishing a dichotomy of both traditional, "premodern" or discrete space—the concept of room (master bedroom and library) and modern space—overlapping, interpenetrating, and loosely defined spaces (living/dining areas and balconies).

House in Mississippi, Laurel, Mississippi. See Color Plate 3.
Design and drawing: Anthony Ames Architect

Anthony Ames Architect

Atlanta, Georgia

Martinelli Residence, Roxbury, Connecticut

Explanation of the Drawing Process and Technique

Up-view axonometric. Color adhesive film on photographic print of ink line drawing.

Purpose of the Drawing

The drawing illustrates the three-dimensional implications of the juxtaposition of the traditionally conceived spaces—bedrooms, library, and kitchen—with the more modern spaces of the living/dining area.

Design Concept

The design strategy synthesizes two attitudes toward residential architecture: The first attitude is static, formal, and public with qualities reminiscent of Renaissance idealism, and the second attitude is dynamic, less formal, and more privately oriented. The major spaces, the living and dining areas, are oriented to the south. They are wrapped and protected from the northern exposure by a thickened "L" element that contains the other, more traditionally conceived spaces—bedrooms, bathrooms, library, and kitchen—and juxtaposes the modern spaces of the living/dining area. The fireplace nestles in the inside corner of the "L" and marks the physical and psychological center of the house.

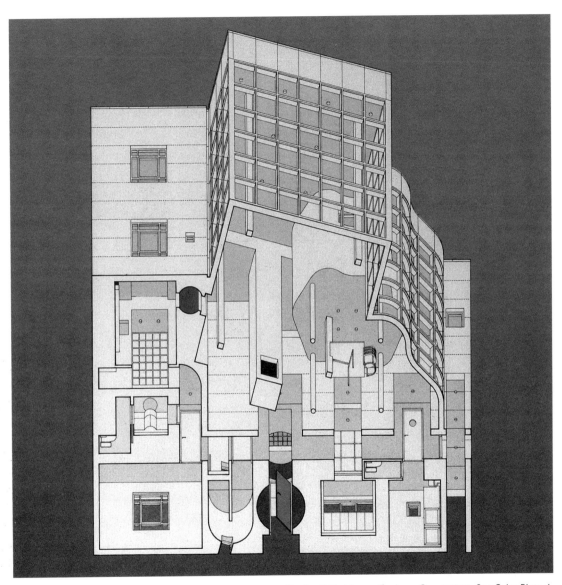

Martinelli Residence, Roxbury, Connecticut. See Color Plate 4.
Design and drawing: Anthony Ames Architect

Atlanta, Georgia

Alpharetta Library, Atlanta, Georgia

Explanation of the Drawing Process and Technique

Computer-generated exploded perspective. Ink plotter on Mylar.

Purpose of the Drawing

The drawing illustrates the three items that are established and emphasized through the choice of materials. The plinth is constructed of a ground-face concrete block that approximates the appearance of a granite base; the roof fascia is made of a gridded metal panel system; and the infill—the walls of the occupiable area of the building—are faced with cementitious panels. A curvilinear glass block wall encloses the browsing area and serves as a buffer between the orientations of the public and private areas.

Design Concept

The building is conceived as a square in plan. It consists of a plinth and a flat roof plane that are separated by a column grid. The edges of the building and the orientation of the column grid acknowledge the site edge. The service areas (support facilities) are treated as poche and occupy one quadrant of the quadripartite plan. The other three-quarters of the plan house the public facilities and are treated in an open, modern, and flexible way. The service quadrant aligns with the entry sequence, which is cranked toward the corner of the site to acknowledge the building's relationship to the intersection of the two streets. A dichotomy is thus created between the closed, room-like qualities of the service area and the open, free-plan nature of the public areas.

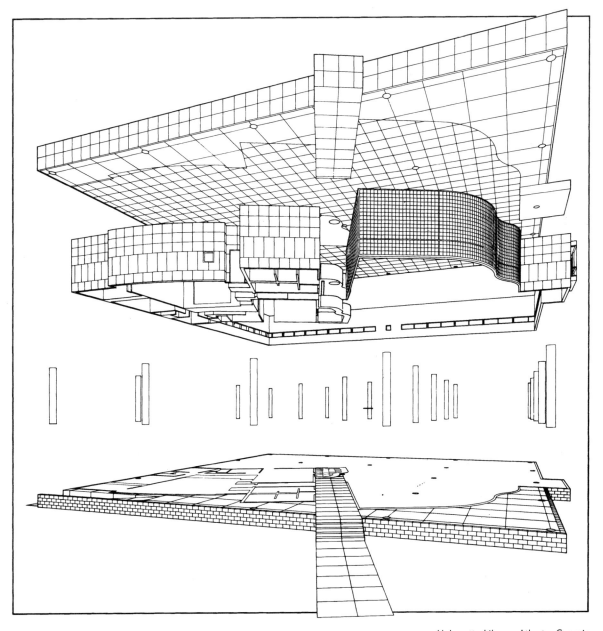

Alpharetta Library, Atlanta, Georgia.
Design and drawing: Anthony Ames Architect
Computer drawing: Alan Brown

Washington, D.C.

Sunshelter Project, New York, New York

Profile

Architecture can function as an art form that affects the cultural formation of our society. As the city is the composite of architecture and the human condition, the relationship between architecture and the city is a primary theme in the designs of Benjamin H. Ames. Following years of study and work in Europe and the United States, Mr. Ames' design concepts often involve issues of cultural identity and spatial perception in the city. In addition to site issues of a project, program and personalities also influence Mr. Ames' design process, which attempts to discover and reveal the essence of each project through architectural expression. Mr. Ames believes that drawings and models are essential tools in the design process. The mere act of building allows the architect to visualize and test different design concepts. While sketches and diagrams respond to cultural, programmatic, and site issues, models remain the purest form of design.

Explanation of the Drawing Process and Technique

A black-and-white aerial photograph is scanned into a software program that can manipulate its image, assigning color to it. Within this aerial photo image, the project's site is highlighted, using a "blur" tool to de-emphasize the site's borders. Tracing paper is placed on the original aerial photo to sketch diagrams. These pen sketches are then scanned into the computer. The image file thus created is given a vibrant color, scaled to fit, and placed on the image of the aerial photo.

Purpose of the Drawing

This image was created as part of a competition entry. Since the entire presentation board was composed on a computer, there was a desire to use various types of media. The image was conceived as a method of integrating hand drawings into a computer layout program. By scanning hand-drawn sketches, software programs are used more as a vehicle than a creation tool. This technique is used to demonstrate how hand-drawn diagrams are essential to Mr. Ames' design process.

Design Concept

As part of the rehabilitation efforts along New York's western waterfront, abandoned piers were planned to provide usable public space. For the Sunshelter Design Competition, Mr. Ames' proposal was to use Pier 54 as a mediating device between the city and the shore. An architectural element, the sunshelter, provides the armature for this mediation to occur. At the urban scale, the pier provides a link to the city by allowing the spatial character of West 14th Street to be extended. The vertical sunshelters flank the extension of the street's space. The diagram overlaid on the aerial photo represents the dense massing of the adjacent neighborhood contrasted by the openness of views on Pier 54.

Sunshelter Project, New York, New York. See Color Plate 5.
Design and drawing: Benjamin H. Ames

Benjamin H. Ames

Washington, D.C.

Sunshelter Project, New York, New York

Explanation of the Drawing Process and Technique

A medium-scale study model is built, with some attention to its detailing. Using controlled studio lights, these models are photographed with a human-scale viewpoint. Photographs of different human figures are scanned. The photographs of the models are scanned into the computer, and the scanned figures are collaged onto the scene. The transparency, sharpness, and motion of these figures can be manipulated to better integrate the figures with the background and to enhance feelings of life and movement.

Purpose of the Drawing

The images represent a type of visualization tool that exists somewhat in the realm of the "real" without becoming too realistic. The obvious flaws in the study model help give the images a certain credibility. The technique is viewed as a way of using computer programs in a secondary role, instead of creating virtual images that exist solely in cyberspace. The image illustrates the pier's ability to accommodate social activities. By integrating individual figures with background photos of the study model, a perception of the space and its activities can be visualized.

Design Concept

Mr. Ames believes that models are an essential tool in the design process. The mere act of building allows the architect to visualize and test different design concepts. While sketches and diagrams respond to cultural, programmatic, and site issues, models remain the purest form of design.

Sunshelter Project, New York, New York. See Color Plates 6 and 7.
Design and drawing: Benjamin H. Ames

Tadao Ando

Tadao Ando Architect & Associates, Osaka, Japan

Church on the Water, Tomamu, Hokkaido, Japan

Profile

Internationally acclaimed Japanese architect Tadao Ando's design integrity lies in his deep interest in geometry, place, and nature. Mr. Ando believes that one of the important roles of architecture is to both recognize and respond to its setting; geometry is the means to realize this, and by doing so, nature will be given a specific kind of order. His architectural interpretation of nature is one in which the elements of light, rain, and wind can be directly sensed by a building's occupants. His fame came in the early 1980s after the successful completion of a number of concrete houses. Mr. Ando's enormous success has led to his being in great demand as a teacher, especially in the United States, where he has taught at Harvard, Columbia, and Yale universities.

Explanation of the Drawing Process and Technique

Transparent perspective and composite section-elevation. The perspective is a line drawing in ink and the section-elevation is a color pencil drawing on paper (1100 mm × 4000 mm).

Purpose of the Drawing

Presentation as well as exploration.

Design Concept

A plateau in the central mountains of Hokkaido, Japan's coldest region, is the setting for this chapel. Nearby are thick stands of wilderness. The entire area is blanketed in green from spring to summer and then transforms, in winter, to an unbroken expanse of white. The chapel plan consists of two—large and small—overlapping squares, and has been created on the shore of an artificial pond created by diverting a nearby stream. A freestanding L-shaped wall wraps around the back of the building and one side of the pond. Approach to the church is made from the back, and entry involves a circuitous route along the freestanding wall. The murmur of water accompanies one's progress, but its source remains hidden, heightening expectations, until one proceeds through the wall and confronts the broad expanse of the pond. Making a 180-degree turn, one ascends a gentle slope to enter a glass-enclosed vestibule, a box of light. Arriving in the chapel itself, one again confronts the pond, whose placid expanse and large cross rising from the water are visible through the glass altar wall. This entire glass wall can slide to the side, opening the church to the pond, which exists purely in its wilderness setting. The sound of water, the fragrance of trees, the song of birds—here, people encounter nature directly.

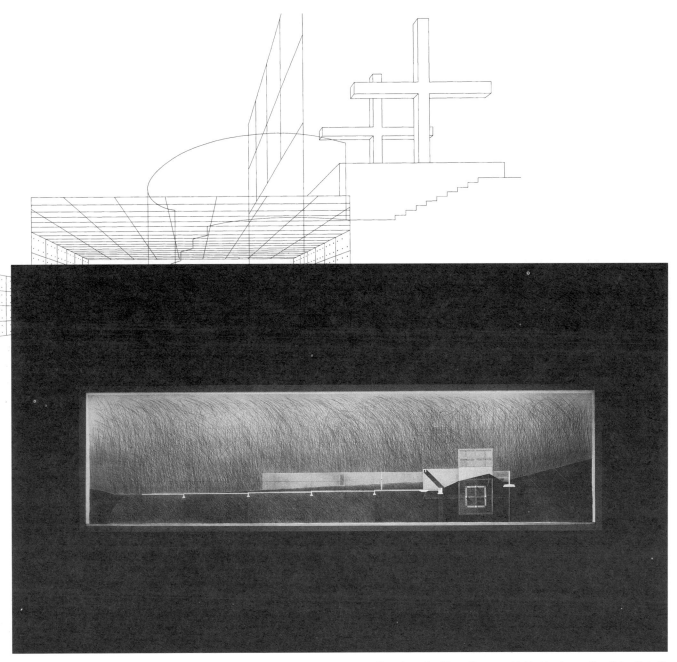

Church on the Water, Tomamu, Hokkaido, Japan. See Color Plate 8.
Design and drawing: Tadao Ando Architect & Associates

Tadao Ando

Tadao Ando Architect & Associates, Osaka, Japan

Church of the Light, Ibaragi, Osaka, Japan

Explanation of the Drawing Process and Technique

Transparent interior perspective and composite plan. The perspective is a line drawing in ink, and the plan rendering is a color pencil drawing on paper (845 mm × 1085 mm).

Purpose of the Drawing

Presentation as well as exploration.

Design Concept

This church is located in a quiet residential suburb of Osaka. It consists of a rectangular volume sliced through at a 15-degree angle by a completely freestanding wall that separates the entrance from the chapel. Light penetrates the profound darkness of this box through a cross, which is cut out of the altar wall. The floor and pews are made of rough scaffolding planks, which are inexpensive and also well suited to the character of the space. Tadao Ando has always used natural materials for parts of a building that come into contact with people's hands or feet, as he is convinced that materials having substance, such as wood or concrete, are invaluable for building, and that it is essentially through the senses that we become aware of architecture. Openings have been limited in this space, for light shows its brilliance only against a backdrop of darkness. Nature's presence is also limited to the element of light and is rendered exceedingly abstract. In responding to such an abstraction, the architecture grows purer. The linear pattern formed on the floor by rays from the sun and a migrating cross of light purely expresses humankind's relationship with nature.

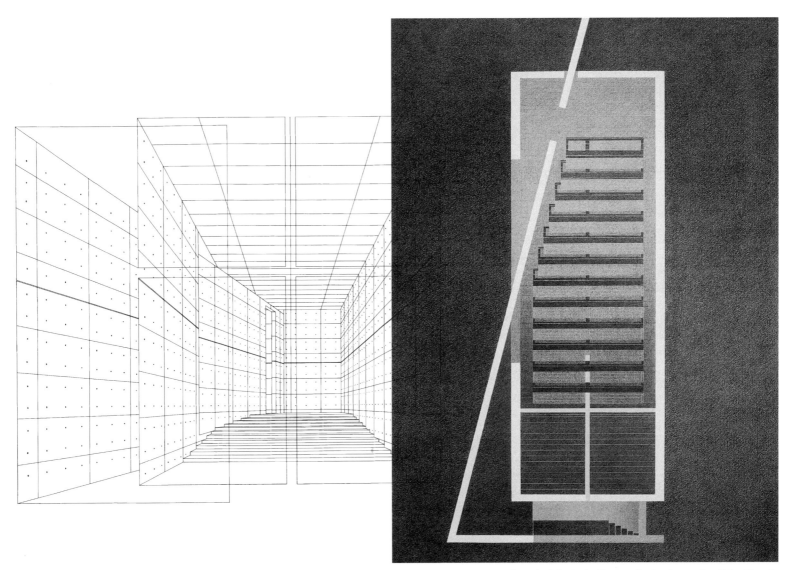

Church of the Light, Ibaragi, Osaka, Japan. See Color Plate 9.
Design and drawing: Tadao Ando Architect & Associates

R. L. Binder, FAIA, Architecture & Planning

Playa del Rey, California

UCLA, Ackerman Student Union Building, Los Angeles, California

Profile

R. L. Binder, FAIA, Architecture & Planning, established in 1979, is a woman-owned architecture firm providing comprehensive planning, programming, and design services. The work of the firm has been widely published and exhibited, and the firm is recognized nationally and internationally as a leading design firm in Southern California. R. L. Binder has created a body of architectural work that is the culmination of focused and informed creative thought. The firm's completed works include large-scale commercial, institutional, and residential projects.

Explanation of the Drawing Process and Technique

Exploded axonometric provides a visual catalog of components composing the reading room space. Rotated axonometric unfolding (time-lapse) view of the reading room seen at once from above and below.

Purpose of the Drawing

These drawings were developed to illustrate design concepts to owners and users, as well as for documentation.

Design Concept

The overall building design incorporates expansion through the "lamination" of 45,000 square feet, in two levels, to the public facades of the 1960 UCLA Student Union. The reading room is sited prominently at the corner of the two "wings," defining and forming the edge of the newly configured Bruin Plaza.

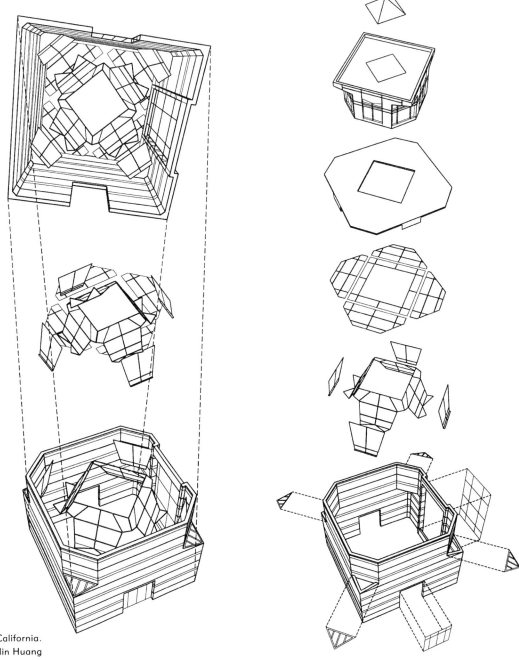

UCLA, Ackerman Student Union Building, Los Angeles, California.
Drawing: Chilin Huang

R. L. Binder, FAIA, Architecture & Planning

Playa del Rey, California

UCLA, Ackerman Student Union Building, Los Angeles, California

Explanation of the Drawing Process and Technique

Shadowed axonometrics emphasizing the elements of the Student Union interpreted in shadow lines (screens, stairs, window frames, etc.). Drawn on AutoCAD.

Purpose of the Drawing

Drawings offer opportunity for shadow study.

Design Concept

Stone tracery, struts, penetration, and rooftop assemblage of arbor, mechanical enclosures, and "pavilions" define and organize.

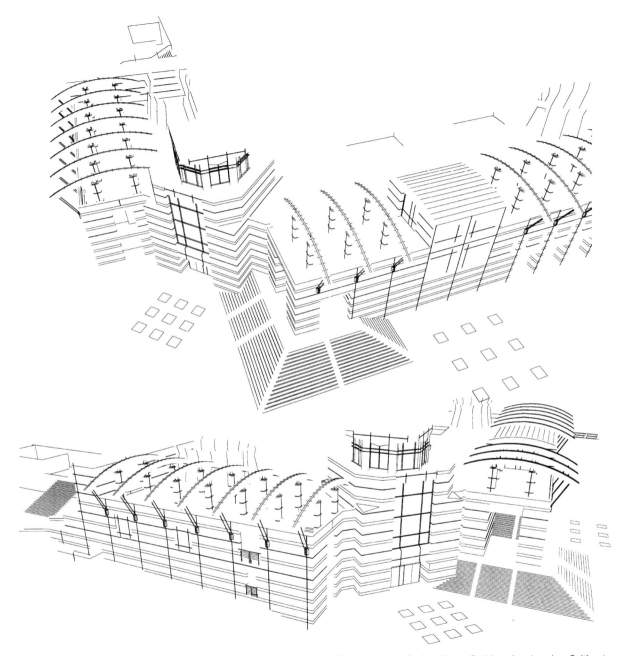

UCLA, Ackerman Student Union Building, Los Angeles, California.
Design and drawing: R. L. Binder, FAIA Architecture & Planning

Eamonn Canniffe

The University of Sheffield, Sheffield, England

Piazza del Foro, Brescia, Italy

Profile

Eamonn Canniffe received his architectural education at Cambridge and Harvard universities. Since his graduation in 1984, he has worked in his native city, principally as a lecturer at Manchester University School of Architecture. He has received awards for collaborative competition work in Davis, California (1988), Perpignan (1991), Atlanta, Georgia (1994), and Liverpool (1994). In 1996, he held a Rome Scholarship in the Fine Arts at the British School in Rome; he currently teaches at the University of Sheffield.

Explanation of the Drawing Process and Technique

The drawing is one of a series of four illustrating episodes from the urban development of Brescia in northern Italy. This panel shows the forum of the Roman town of Brixia, is executed in watercolor, transfer printing, and collage on paper, and measures 28"×20". The general plan of the city is shown as a painted panel over the lower right-hand corner, while the existing plan of the piazza is contrasted with a red painted plan of the Roman forum to the left, with the center occupied by an image of the ancient bronze statue of Victory. Archaeological fragments and in situ reconstructions are illustrated as superimposed marble fragments, with representations in frontal axonometric projection.

Purpose of the Drawing

The focus of the drawings of which this is an example is the description of Italian urban space, and the formal tensions between space and object. This is explored through representations of urban space and the effects of illusionism, theatricality, urban layering, and typological transformations. The broad purpose of this study is the exploration of an element of urban architecture that the 20th century has had difficulty in emulating. Successful public space has always contained representational and communicative elements, but this seems impossible to achieve in our time. With the perceived fragmentation of urban society into distinct groups with few common values other than protection and privacy, where does that leave the public arena?

Design Concept

The projection method chosen for each drawing is intended to complement the period from which the piazza originates, to emphasize the link between spatial representations of the city and the constructed representation of a society in a public space.

Piazza del Foro, Brescia, Italy. See Color Plate 10.
Drawing: Eamonn Canniffe.

Douglas Darden

Denver, Colorado

Oxygen House, A Near Triptych on the Act of Breathing

Profile

Douglas Darden, a native of Denver, Colorado, studied industrial design at the Parsons School of Design and received his master's degree in architecture from Harvard University. Awarded the Prize for Architecture from the American Academy in Rome in 1988, he went on to lecture extensively, both nationally and internationally. In 1992, Princeton Architectural Press published a collection of his work, *Condemned Building*. Mr. Darden taught design at Columbia University, Catholic University, the New Jersey Institute of Technology, and held a tenure-track position at the University of Colorado's School of Architecture. He saw architecture as fundamentally a tool of inquiry into how we live, revealing the narrative quality of place and program. Mr. Darden died in 1996.

Explanation of the Drawing Process and Technique

The line drawings are ink on Mylar film. The chiaroscuro drawing for the anatomical section is graphite, graphite powder, gouache, and pastel on Stonehenge paper (from *Condemned Building*, Princeton Architectural Press, 1992).

Purpose of the Drawing

The "Dis/continuous Genealogies" represent a composite conceptualization of iconography, structure, formal composition, and program of the architectural project.

Design Concept

Oxygen House is perched on a depressed flood plain north-northwest of Frenchman's Bend, Mississippi. The structure was designed for Burnden Abraham, an ex-train signalman, who must live in an oxygen tent. In the early spring of 1979, after torrential rains, the railroad tracks on which Abraham worked were flooded. They were never fully repaired. The following summer, during a routine operation, Abraham suffered a collapsed lung when a train jumped the track and metal debris punctured his right lung. Three years later, the railroad company put the property up for sale. Abraham purchased the plot where he had once worked. He requested that his house be built over the scene of his near-fatal accident. Abraham also requested that he finally be entombed in the house.

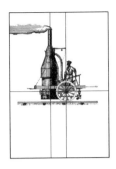
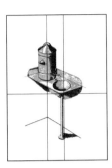

Dis/continuous Genealogies
American Civil War Engraving
Caboose Water Cooler and Basin
Westinghouse Train Brake
Hindenburg Zeppelin
Composite Ideogram

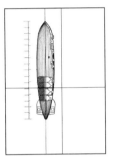
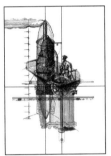

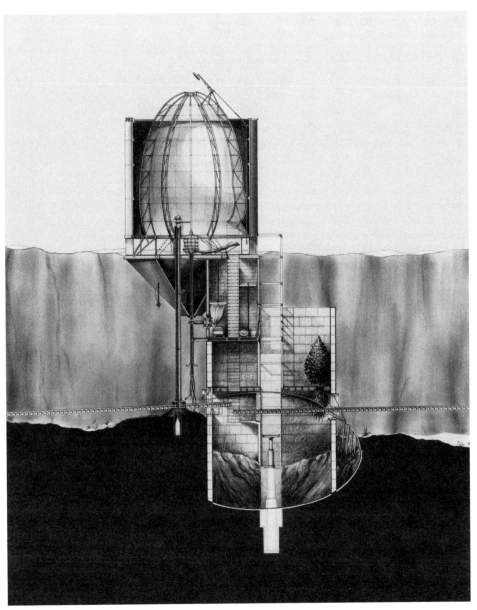

Oxygen House, A Near Triptych on the Act of Breathing
Design and drawing: Douglas Darden

John J. Desmond, FAIA

John J. Desmond & Associates, Baton Rouge, Louisiana

Natchez, Mississippi

Profile

John J. Desmond, FAIA, has had an active practice as an architect for more than 40 years. He has been a member of the A.I.A. (American Institute of Architects) Regional Urban Design Assistant Teams, assisting cities in urban design issues. His articles and drawings have been often published in the *A.I.A. Journal*. The firm has won more than 30 A.I.A. and other design awards, including six national awards. Mr. Desmond has also received the Mayor-President's Excellence in the Arts Award (Baton Rouge, Louisiana, 1994). In the design of buildings, he has especially been aware of site characteristics as a major contribution to the project.

Explanation of the Drawing Process and Technique

The drawing shown here is of Natchez, Mississippi, and combines a regional view of the Natchez area and its unique topography with sketches of the individual buildings in their approximate locations. The drawing is done in India ink using professional pens and is about 30"×20".

Purpose of the Drawing

The purpose of this drawing was for publication, giving a summary view for an article on the Annual Festival of Natchez, Mississippi.

Design Concept

The design concept was to show the general topography of a city that was situated in a flood-free area on the loess hills along the Mississippi River, the main highway of commerce in the 19th century, and to demonstrate how settlement on the high grounds developed into a unique collection of architectural treasures.

Natchez, Mississippi.
Drawing: John J. Desmond

Peter Edgeley for Daryl Jackson Architects

Melbourne, Australia

Office Tower, 120 Collins Street, Melbourne, Australia

Profile

Peter Edgeley qualified as an architect in the United Kingdom and now works mainly as an illustrator and painter in Australia. He has received awards at the annual exhibitions of the American Society of Architectural Perspectivists and has been an invited exhibitor with the Illustrators Society of Japan. He has also exhibited at the Royal College of Art in the United Kingdom, as well as in his adopted home in Australia. His work as an architect and illustrator has received commendation at international level. He is currently combining CAD and digital work with conventional drawing and painting.

Explanation of the Drawing Process and Technique

Photomontage, rendering of proposed building on a photographic print. The site boundaries were defined first. The essential geometry of the view was analyzed—i.e., vanishing points and horizon line. The tower design was then plotted on tracing paper using the same camera position, height, and center of view. The linework was then transferred onto the photographic print using a Chinagraph pencil, and the glazing areas were airbrushed in. Finally, using mixed media of acrylic and gouache, the structure was rendered on top.

Purpose of the Drawing

The drawing was made to show the insertion of a new tower within the existing city fabric.

Design Concept

The sketch design was for an office tower located over a mixed-use area with a central glass-covered atrium. A photomontage was needed to show this in the context of the overall cityscape.

Office Tower, 120 Collins Street, Melbourne, Australia. See Color Plate 11.
Design: Daryl Jackson Architects, Australia
Drawing: Peter Edgeley, Australia

Peter Edgeley for Daryl Jackson Architects

Melbourne, Australia

Sega World, Darling Harbor, Sydney, Australia

Explanation of the Drawing Process and Technique

Photomontage, acrylic paint and airbrush on black card (20"×15"). The sky tones and the foreground water were airbrushed in first, followed by the basic building forms painted over the top. Video screens were then montaged in and further airbrush highlights added last.

Purpose of the Drawing

The drawing was made to show the insertion of an electronic environment.

Design Concept

Sega World was looking at a proposal for a game and multimedia center in Sydney. The design scheme and presentation for the project convey the image of an electronic environment and activities related to video screens.

Sega World, Darling Harbor, Sydney, Australia. See Color Plate 12.
Design: Daryl Jackson Architects, Australia
Drawing: Peter Edgeley, Australia

Melbourne, Australia

Piazza and Ferry Terminal near Sydney Opera House, Sydney, Australia

Explanation of the Drawing Process and Technique

Photomontage, rendering of a new proposal on an aerial site photograph. The scale and extent of the design were first mapped out and sketched on tracing paper over the aerial site photograph. The line drawing was then transferred onto the photographic print and rendered with airbrush, using acrylic paint and gouache.

Purpose of the Drawing

The intention of this finished photomontage was to propose a design scheme that creates a public piazza by relocating the ferry terminals.

Design Concept

The proposed sketch design for the site near the Sydney Opera House suggests relocation of an existing ferry terminal and creation of a public piazza. The design scheme and presentation for the project convey the landscaped environment in the context of the overall site and surroundings.

Piazza and Ferry Terminal near Sydney Opera House, Sydney, Australia.
See Color Plates 13 and 14.
Design: Greg-Scott-Young/EMTB Architects, Australia
Drawing: Peter Edgeley, Australia

Evans Vettori Architects, Derbyshire, England

Cambridge Mediathèque

Profile

Robert Evans formed Evans Vettori Architects with designer Mariangela Vettori in 1995. He specialises in introducing imaginative contemporary architecture into historic settings. The practice's work has received awards and has been widely published thanks to the valuable experience it gained working on such projects as Stansted Airport with Foster & Partners, and the Hotel du Departement in Marseilles with Will Alsop. Evans has lectured and taught extensively, and is currently visiting tutor at Sheffield School of Architecture. Evans Vettori are architects for Nottingham Trent University School of Art and Design.

Explanation of the Drawing Process and Technique

The medium is ink on tracing paper, bringing disparate visual elements into the same single-point perspective. The figures were drawn by Nigel Rayner and then pasted on, with a fragment of imperial Rome on the ceiling. The microchip inner wall was traced from a photograph of scientists working on a large scale tabletop prototype. The video screen was based on an illustration from "Mondo 2000." As a final touch, splashes of colour were added with Pantone film.

Purpose of the Drawing

The purpose was to illustrate the implications of a possible new hybrid building material that combines the permanence and loadbearing capacity of brickwork with the IT transfer capability of a silicon microchip. The drawing investigates a future where man and machine are intertwined within a structure which has its roots in Britain's medieval past.

Design Concept

In the future there will be a new hybrid material, part structure and part electronic matrix. The project investigates a shift in the balance between fabric, people, and information technology. Instead of being diametrically opposed, they are complimentary—users will literally plug themselves into the building fabric to access cyberspace. The monumental facade leans towards the town, revealing glimpses of computing apparatus within.

Cambridge Mediathèque
Design and drawing: Robert Evans

Robert J. Fakelmann

Associate Professor, Louisiana Tech University, Louisiana

Anthromorphs

Profile

Robert J. Fakelmann is a registered architect in Texas and an associate professor of architecture at Louisiana Tech University. His drawings have been exhibited in university galleries and his projects have received citations in several design competitions. His work has also been published in *GA Houses* and has been presented at national design conferences. He currently has a studio in Ruston, Louisiana.

Explanation of the Drawing Process and Technique

The original ink-on-Mylar line drawing combines elevations, axonometrics, and aspects of plan drawing into a single overlay composition. The drawing was reproduced into a full sized 1:1 photo mechanical transfer. Architectural model photographs were digitized with the aid of a Xerox color copier and added to complete the composition. The resulting hybrid collage consists of ink drawings, photographic model imagery, black tape, and colored paper.

Purpose of the Drawing

The drawing was produced as one in a series of images for gallery exhibition. The hybrid approach represents a quick technique for adding three-dimensional imagery and color to black-and-white line drawings.

Design Concept

The project represented in this composition is part of a hypothetical study that examines the translation and interpretation of anthropomorphic form in architectural design. Kinetic features are illustrated with varied line weight in order to animate the form's anthropomorphic character.

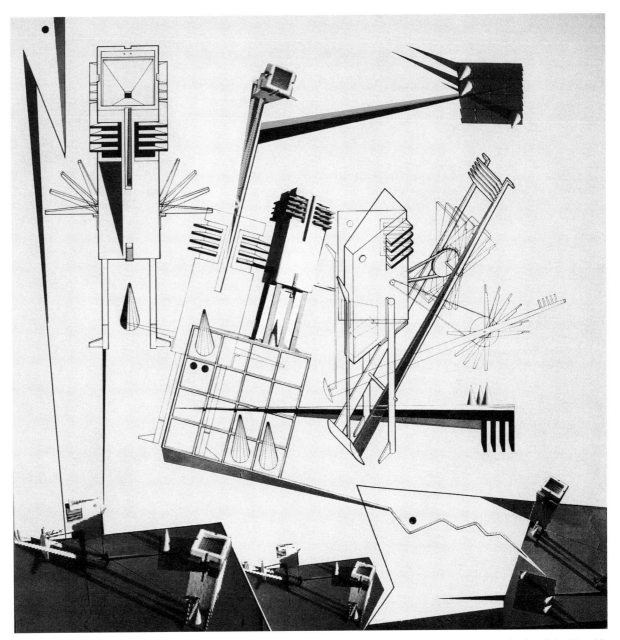

Anthromorphs. See Color Plate 15.
Design and drawing: Robert J. Fakelmann

Robert J. Fakelmann

Associate Professor, Louisiana Tech University, Louisiana

The His and Her House

Explanation of the Drawing Process and Technique

The original ink-on-Mylar line drawing is an oblique axonometric elevation. The drawing was reproduced into a full sized 1:1 PMT. Architectural model photographs were digitized with the aid of a Xerox color copier and added to complete the composition. The resulting hybrid collage consists of an ink line drawing, photographic model imagery, and black tape.

Purpose of the Drawing

The drawing was produced as one in a series of images for gallery exhibition. The hybrid approach represents a quick technique for adding three-dimensional imagery and color to black-and-white line drawings.

Design Concept

The project represented in this composition is a residence designed for a couple who live and work in their home environment. The ground level and first floor are programmed living spaces, while the upper level is divided into two discrete work spaces.

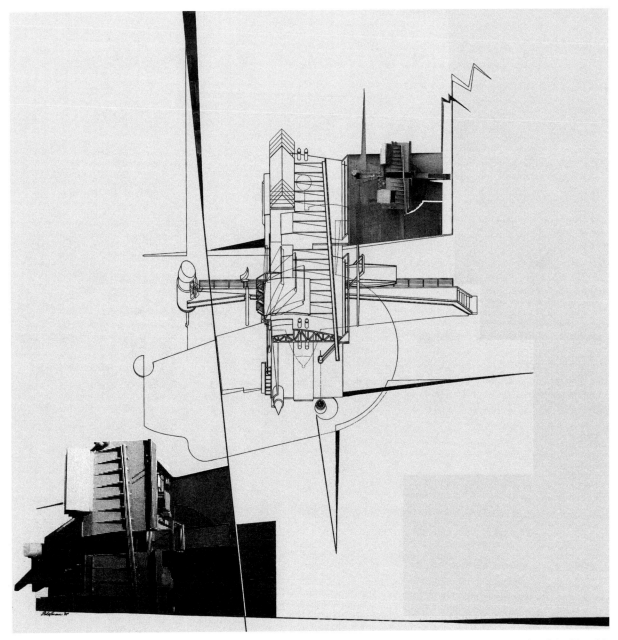

The His and Her House. See Color Plate 16.
Design and drawing: Robert J. Fakelmann

Richard B. Ferrier, FAIA

Professor, The University of Texas at Arlington

GBC Douglas Lake House, Lake Texamco, Texas

Profile

Richard B. Ferrier, FAIA, is an educator and practicing architect from Dallas, Texas, who was elected to the College of Fellows of the American Institute of Architects in 1993. He is a professor of architecture at the University of Texas at Arlington School of Architecture and serves as a consultant for the School of Architecture at Prairie View A & M University. His drawings and architecture with Firm X have been widely published and recognized, having received more than 75 professional awards.

Explanation of the Drawing Process and Technique

Photo-sketch, spatial representation through a combination of photographs of construction and hand drawing of created perspective (from photographs). During construction, photographic snapshots were made of interior spaces to document on-site progress. The photographs were spliced together, with the remaining perspective completed as a graphite drawing.

Purpose of the Drawing

This photo-sketch drawing is a method of visualizing the completed space. This process is informative for the owner, as well as for the construction team.

Design Concept

The client had purchased and used an old cabin located on this site, which was destroyed. The architects elected to recall the existing plan and respect the original dimensions of the structure. With this strategy, they did not block previously existing views to the lake by adjacent property owners. The original plan was simple and direct. One enters the kitchen/dining area, traverses a few steps down to the living room and fireplace, then goes out through glass doors to a wooden deck overlooking the lake.

KITCHEN · BREAKFAST · BALCONY

GBC Douglas Lake House, Lake Texamco, Texas. See Color Plate 17.
Drawing: Richard B. Ferrier
Photographer: C. Kuhner

Richard B. Ferrier, FAIA

Professor, The University of Texas at Arlington

Windows and Fragments: Karl Friedrich Schinkel

Explanation of the Drawing Process and Technique

Conceptual drawing; graphite, watercolor, photographic film images, and metals on 300# Arches watercolor paper 22"×30".

Purpose of the Drawing

This watercolor drawing is a method of exploring conceptual ideas. Considerations and discoveries from this process improve this designer's own work as an architect.

Design Concept

Because of the division of Germany as a result of World War II, architects and historians in the West were denied access to the work of Karl Friedrich Schinkel. With new research and careful study of this architect's accomplishments, the significance of his influence on modern architects, such as Mies van der Rohe, is becoming more clear. This drawing brings together numerous images and implications of architectonic notions based on Schinkel's formalistic design components. The drawing is a tribute to the significance and influence of this architect.

Windows and Fragments: Karl Friedrich Schinkel. See Color Plate 18.
Drawing: Richard B. Ferrier, FAIA

Form:uLA/Bryan Cantley + Kevin O'Donnell

Bryan Cantley, Santa Ana, California + Kevin O'Donnell, Los Angeles, California

Through the Looking Glass Housing

Profile

Bryan Cantley and Kevin O'Donnell have been working collaboratively on opposite coasts for the past five years. The two have established a virtual partnership that has explored mainly theoretical analogs via electronic communication. The studio Form:uLA is founded on the idea of transforming entities of movement, technology, and spirit of place via the language of the machine. Recently, the two have started to explore these ideas via small built projects and installations.

Explanation of the Drawing Process and Technique

Individual study models were were photographed with a digital camera, then enhanced using Photoshop. The large final model was photographed, scanned, and color-transformed with Photoshop. A large background featuring models and symbols was prepared; then, the entire image was imported into QuarkXPress. Text and HUD symbology were constructed in Quark, then applied to the background. Other scanned images were then layered on top of the existing composite, using Quark. The image was then transferred to slide form.

Purpose of the Drawing

This poster was originally constructed as an advertising display for an academic architectural exhibition/installation in the spring of 1997. Seen as a composite of the design process, images ranged from original concept models to schematic studies and post-design graphic confirmations.

Design Concept

Developed as one-half of an interpretation of the Lewis Carroll books *Alice in Wonderland* and *Through the Looking Glass*, the projects were follies attempting to translate the physical components of a book: cover, page, and text. Hypothetical membranes between spaces of a chessboard were conceived as transformational planes, thus promoting a wall structure that houses a moving virtual cube, which holographically represents interpretations of individual chapters of the text.

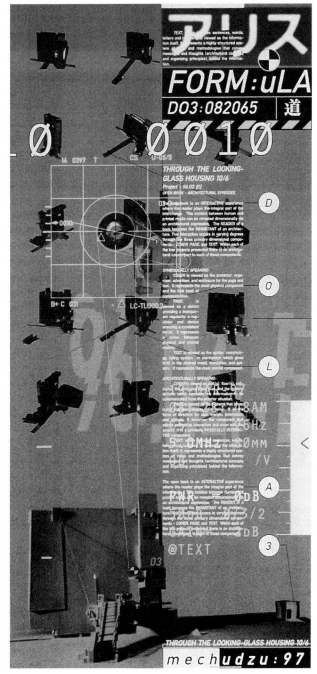

Through the Looking Glass Housing. See Color Plate 19.
Design: Bryan Cantley + Kevin O'Donnell
Photos: Jan Bruins + Bryan Cantley

Form:uLA/Bryan Cantley + Kevin O'Donnell

Bryan Cantley, Santa Ana, California + Kevin O'Donnell, Los Angeles, California

Outhouse Prototype [urban variant] No. 93.7, Poster No. 2.

Explanation of the Drawing Process and Technique

Whereas the vast majority of the team's projects have been collaboratively produced despite 3000 miles of geographic separation, this project stands alone as the only drawing they have produced together while in the same location. This drawing is a three-color silkscreen printed image. Each layer of color was cut from blockout film and photos were shot as half-tone images. The cutouts and photos were then composed on a sheet of acetate and burned onto a screen coated with a light-sensitive material. Each screen prints a color carefully registered and layered on top of the previous one until all three have been printed.

Purpose of the Drawing

This poster was produced as a handout for an installation/exhibition in San Francisco at the 1994 International Making Cities Livable Conference. The exhibition consisted of six 20"×30" panels. The four center panels were intended to read as a whole and the two end panels were intended to both read as part of the whole composition and stand on their own. The entire series of six panels were two-color silkscreened drawings. The posters were created by adding a third color layer to both exhibition end panels. This is the second of two posters.

Design Concept

The project represented on this poster is a kinetic public restroom facility located in New York City and Los Angeles. A completely self-sustainable facility, the Outhouse Prototype constructs itself when called into service and deconstructs itself following each paid use. Occupation, movement, and interactive interior/exterior video display are required in order to transform the outhouse from street sculpture to architecture.

Outhouse Prototype [urban variant] No. 93.7, Poster No. 2. See Color Plate 20.
Design and drawing: Bryan Cantley + Kevin O'Donnell

Thomas P. Gallagher

Denver, Colorado

(New) Welfare Island Colony, Roosevelt Island, New York (Academic Project)

Profile

Thomas P. Gallagher is an architect living in Denver, Colorado. He is interested in the liberation of the unconscious in the design process and intuitively guided collage and montage as design precedent. The image shown here is part of a final graduate design studio at the University of Nebraska in 1993.

Explanation of the Drawing Process and Technique

An artifact (model) was constructed from a mannequin and a typewriter. Photography, rescaling, and xerographic manipulation of text passages, the model, and the real site combined to produce this image. The technique was hand collage, which was subsequently scanned and used as an underlay for computer modeling.

Purpose of the Drawing

The montage was intended to depict an urban scenario. Like a Surrealist collage, it defines an unreal event (floating naked over the city) in an entirely realistic way. The drawing became the point of departure for this student design project on Roosevelt Island.

Design Concept

This project began with the random act of selecting a mannequin's thigh. The process concerned itself with the chance connections brought about by the selection and recombination of fragments. An object (a mannequin's thigh) became the topic of personal desire or fetish, providing at once a thematic source and formal study: a form-armature for the architecture to follow.

(New) Welfare Island Colony, Roosevelt Island, New York (Academic Project). See Color Plate 21.
Design and drawing: Thomas P. Gallagher

Gilbert Gorski

Lincolnwood, Illinois

Philadelphia Commercial Project, Philadelphia

Profile

Gilbert Gorski began his career as an architect. He was the project designer for numerous buildings, including the world headquarters for McDonald's Corporation in Oak Brook, Illinois, and the Oceanarium, a major addition to the John G. Shedd Aquarium in Chicago. Mr. Gorski has also served as a studio professor and has lectured at many of the universities for architectural studies in the Chicago area. His award-winning drawings and paintings have been included in a host of publications on architecture and illustration. The Art Institute of Chicago has acquired his work for its permanent collection. In 1990, the American Society of Architectural Perspectivists awarded Mr. Gorski the nation's highest singular honor in architectural illustration, the Hugh Ferriss Memorial Prize. Since 1989, Mr. Gorski has had his own practice, specializing in architectural illustration.

Explanation of the Drawing Process and Technique

Exterior ground-level night view perspective superimposed on plan footprints. Color pencil and airbrush on gray illustration board.

Purpose of the Drawing

This is part of a set of three images. The purpose of the drawing was to promote the project to prospective tenants and to convey the compelling nature of this building type, an urban entertainment complex. Depicting a foggy rainy night enhances the dramatic character of the building. Meant to convey a "Blade Runner" feel, the layering of plan and sections with the perspective creates the feeling of a mechanical drawing of a machine for entertainment.

Design Concept

The building was concieved as a "machine for entertainment." Organized around a central atrium or "electric canyon," the neon signage, moving message board, and giant video boards become the architecture. Retail spaces extend vertically and horizontally and "intertwine" to redefine the traditional concept of a vertical retail center. The ultimate goal of the design was to create a branded iconic image for the urban entertainment complex that could be developed in numerous locations worldwide.

Philadelphia Commercial Project, Philadelphia. See Color Plate 22.
Design: Dan Mies for Ellerbe Becket, Inc., Los Angeles
Rendering: Gilbert Gorski

Gordon Grice

Gordon Grice + Associates, Toronto, Canada

Art Deco Family Entertainment Center, Antwerp, Belgium

Profile

Gordon Grice, OAA, MRAIC, is an architect and illustrator based in Toronto, serving an international clientele. His drawings have been published and exhibited around the world. Mr. Grice is the editor of five books on architectural illustration and is president emeritus of the American Society of Architectural Illustrators.

Explanation of the Drawing Process and Technique

The drawing is executed in ruled ink line on Mylar film. A variety of Rapidograph jewel-tipped nibs was used with fast-drying latex ink. Individual elements of the drawing were first roughed in pencil, then enlarged or reduced on a photocopier and taped together. A final pencil rough was made from this assemblage before being traced onto Mylar.

Purpose of the Drawing

The drawing was intended to give some idea of the complexity and excitement of the space and a feeling for the thematic treatment. It accompanied a master plan proposal prepared by Forrec Ltd., a firm specializing in the design of recreation and entertainment facilities.

Design Concept

The proposed facility was to be located in a shopping center on the outskirts of Antwerp in an area with a rich Art Deco tradition, so the idea of an Art Deco theme was contextually appropriate. The elements of the drawing and overall illustration style are meant to evoke a sense of the Art Deco theme, while not being too descriptive of the actual space (which had yet to be designed). Although the drawing is largely a two-dimensional composition, some depth is suggested by overlapping objects, changes in scale, and the extension of some elements outside the drawing frame.

Art Deco Family Entertainment Center, Antwerp, Belgium.
Drawing: Gordon Grice

Harlan Hambright/InSite for Kohn Pedersen Fox, Architects

Harlan Hambright/InSite, St. Simons Island, Georgia

AARP Addition, Washington, DC

Profile

Harlan Hambright received a bachelor of architecture with honors from the University of Tennessee in 1976. He started his career as an architectural photographer during a recession. Later, he moved to Washington, DC, and became very active as a photographer for various agencies, including the U.S. State Department. He was also actively involved with the National Building Museum and was its in-house photographer for two years. In the mid-1980s, he pioneered techniques for superimposing model photographs into site photographs and saw the advantages of driving the process with three-dimensional computer modeling techniques. This technology allowed him to move to St. Simons Island, Georgia in 1990, where he works in three-dimensional modeling and graphic design, and publishes a weekly magazine. He is also a member of the Glynn County School Board, where he is a proponent of technology use in education.

Explanation of the Drawing Process and Technique

A hidden line wire frame was generated to match the perspective of the site photograph. The wire frame was dropped into the scanned site image and rendered with textures copied from the existing building. A rendering software program was used for all paint and rendering procedures on a Macintosh platform.

Purpose of the Drawing

The drawing was created for the client to show the new proposal in the context of the existing built environment.

Design Concept

An addition to an earlier development, this massive project had to fit into its site, surrounded by older buildings. The three-dimensional model was "painted" with colors and textures copied from the bit of the existing building that was visible in the site photograph.

InSite™

AARP Addition, Washington, DC. See Color Plate 23.
Drawing: Harlan Hambright/InSite

Hemingway + Associates, San Francisco, California

San Francisco Waterfront Competition (SFO-001)

Profile

Hemingway + Associates is an architectural firm engaged in several global project types. Erik M. Hemingway, principal, received his bachelor of architecture from California Polytechnic State University in San Luis Obispo and a master of science degree in advanced architectural design at Columbia University in New York. Recent design honors include Architectural League of New York Young Architect in 1996, and a 44th Annual Progressive Architecture Award Citation in 1997. He is an instructor of architectural design at the University of California, Berkeley.

Explanation of the Drawing Process

Executed on bond paper, Xerox collage, and ink and overlaid with red photographic film, the piece measures 60" long by 40" high.

Purpose of the Drawing

Drawing is a hybrid of photocollage, drawing, and conceptual and theoretical information on the impact of a future large-scale theoretical urban proposal for the San Francisco Waterfront Competition (SFO-001).

Design Concept

This project revitalizes a decaying San Francisco waterfront by interlinking it with a technologically advanced aerial transport/shipping depot and global computer access networks, creating a physical and technological internet freeway. The physical internet zone is proposed through construction of suspended bridges that span the Embarcadero thoroughfare and move outward to shipping docks, using existing pedestrian and transportation systems as a guide map. This construction then acts as an express ground freeway off-ramp that injects itself directly to waiting ships and the sea, echoing San Francisco's maritime origins. This physical interlink is harnessed with computer technology, which maps the surrounding airspace, creating an internet freeway that enables air travel directly into the city. With the import of air traffic, the architecture that emerges is based purely on necessity, implementing this new city configuration. After further technological advances to fully implement and complete this revitalization, new structural adaptations will be possible once the comprehensive long-term view is in place. San Francisco's internet freeway serves as a prototype for other satellites worldwide, creating a global network of information and physical exchange.

San Francisco Waterfront Competition (SFO-001). See Color Plate 24.
Design and drawing: Erik M. Hemingway

HNTB Architecture

Alexandria, Virginia

McGhee Tyson Airport, Knoxville, Tennessee

Profile

As one of the nation's leaders in the design of airports, sports facilities and convention centers, HNTB Architecture has developed substantial expertise in large-scale projects that have a significant impact on their respective regions and urban fabric. In spite of the large size of most of the firm's projects, all aspects of the design are developed to produce an architecture that responds to the region, the city, and the individual. Within the design studio, emphasis is placed on a collegial environment that encourages active collaboration, enabling these large projects to develop with attention to detail without sacrificing the relationship to larger-scale issues. Urban issues are examined and studied, and simultaneously, materiality and detail are considered. Thus, it is the firm's philosophy that every project should be an authentic response to the regional characteristics and idiosyncrasies of its particular place and culture. HNTB uses a variety of media as visual tools to describe the nature of the architectural ideas that evolve. Instead of strictly using one specific type of graphic technique, the office constantly investigates new ways of mixing a variety of media, both electronic and hand-wrought. It is the belief that an assortment of exploratory media is necessary to fully study, understand, and convey the possibilities of design alternatives.

Explanation of the Drawing Process and Technique

Large-scale models are built with attention to detail and materiality. Using controlled studio lights, these models are photographed with a human-scale viewpoint. Entourage elements, such as people in airports, are photographed. The photographs of the models and entourage are scanned into the computer. The entourage elements are cropped from their original background, and the resultant images are collaged into the model images. Their number, size, and orientation are manipulated, often using the same figure more than once. The transparency, sharpness, and motion of these figures can be manipulated to better integrate the figures with the background.

Purpose of the Drawing

The principal uses of these images involve the client and the design studio. These images offer the client presentation media that communicates the design concepts being developed. Within the design studio, such images can effectively respond to design questions that are part of the design process. Thus, issues concerning scale, light, and materiality can better be studied.

Design Concept

This design studio believes strongly in the creation of models as an essential tool in the design process. The process of building both physical and computer models allows the designer to test design concepts, engage "real" issues concerning the project, and better visualize the design's possibilities.

McGhee Tyson Airport, Knoxville, Tennessee. See Color Plates 25 and 26.
Drawing: HNTB Architecture

San Francisco, California

Langmaid Residence, Oakland, California

Profile

Steven and Cathi House and their associates endeavor to create beauty, serenity, and amazement in their work and in the process of architecture. They find their greatest inspiration in the subtleties of each site and in the deepest recesses of their clients' souls—and with intimate analysis, they discover how to mold each project into a unique environment that embodies magic and harmony. In each project, they find new opportunities to lift themselves and their clients to a higher level of perception of the world—not through the latest technology, but through their skillful manipulation of form, light, and texture.

Recognized for their innovative work, house+house has designed projects ranging from custom homes throughout the San Francisco Bay area, the Sierra Nevada mountains, Los Angeles, and Hawaii, to state-of-the-art retail facilities, to a Caribbean island resort. The firm has received numerous design awards and its work has been published extensively. Steven and Cathi House have co-authored "Mediterranean Indigenous Architecture—Timeless Solutions for the Human Habit," a major exhibition that has traveled throughout the United States. The poetic quality of their work derives from the simpler side of life, such as the magic sparkle of sunlight raking across a textured wall.

Explanation of the Drawing Process and Technique

Plan, elevation, and section composite. Pencil, graphite, pastel chalks, and Prismacolor on vellum, 32"×32". The drawing is composed to best define the project within the framework of a single drawing. Specific images were chosen to illustrate the spatial relationships of rooms to each other and to the site. The drawing is rendered in strong earth tones to express the actual colors of the materials.

Purpose of the Drawing

The drawing serves three purposes: a record of the conceptual ideas behind the design for the architect, a gift and a remembrance of the process for the client, and a document for future publication.

Design Concept

The concept of the house began as a diagram for dividing the site into a series of indoor/outdoor spaces in terms of their functions and relationships to sun, views, and privacy. Two intersecting wings are linked together with a series of circular regulating elements. Through the articulation of mass and use of contrasting materials and colors, the house respects the history and traditional atmosphere of the neighborhood.

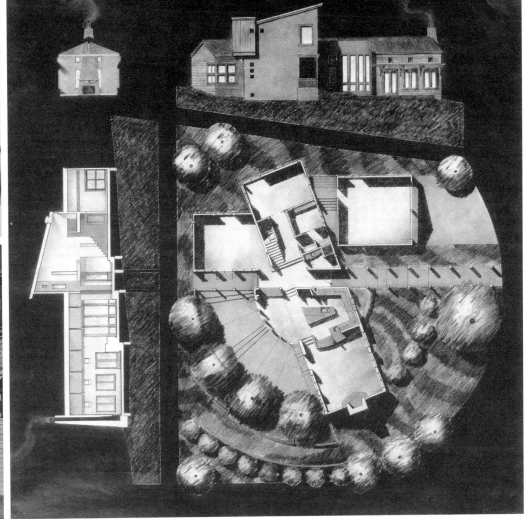

Langmaid Residence, Oakland, California. See Color Plate 27.
Architects: house+house
Drawing: David Haun

San Francisco, California

Suri Residence, Tarzana, California

Explanation of the Drawing Process and Technique

Plan, elevations, and details composite. Pencil and graphite on vellum, 32"×54". The rendering showcases the character of the building through the representation of several of its defining elements. The plan and front elevation dominate the drawing to express the overall formality of the design. Interior elevations and smaller details ring the edge of the drawing to provide a texture of scale and show off the attention to detail within the actual house. The technique of pencil on vellum, both hardline and graphite shadowing, is meant to lend a classical and stately air to the overall composition.

Purpose of the Drawing

The drawing serves three purposes: a record of the conceptual ideas behind the design for the architect, a gift and a remembrance of the process for the client, and a document for future publication.

Design Concept

The genesis of the house was the client's desires for grandeur, symmetry, and spaciousness. All programmed spaces and their sizes were specifically identified and laid out between architect and client. The design that followed from this program was based on a rigid formality of spatial organization and a selection of materials that would best reflect the eminence of such a building.

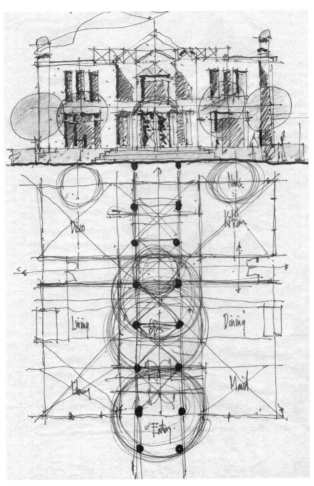

Sketch: Steven House

Suri Residence, Tarzana, California.
Architects: house+house
Drawing: Michael Baushke

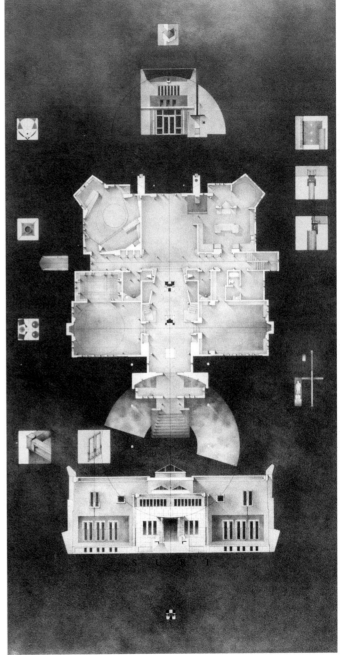

the hut

kevinkennedy/terryvickers, Charlotte, North Carolina

codename: techno-nerd (dayclub w.d. phase one)

Profile

Two themes are always prevalent in the hut's work. The first is the importance of computer technology, which is used not only for design and visualization, but also as a tool that leaves its imprint on the formal language of a project and then allows those forms to be built. The second is the importance of the experiential aspects of architecture. An extrapolation of computer technology reveals that future architecture will be required only to accommodate bodily functions, because the computer will simulate or modify everything else. Therefore, movement, parallax, and an exceedingly tactile, peripherally audible, heightened visual environment that pushes the senses to the threshold of pain is created to affirm the things that this evolving life negates.

Explanation of the Drawing Process and Technique

A "kit of parts" becomes the genesis for this project—concerned only with the design agenda and the collaborative nature of assembly—the techno-nerd's space is formed. The models are of ideas, with no distinct scale and no discernible parts, just sporadic flashes of varied levels of occupation. The ideas of the physical models are transformed into three-dimensional models with Form-Z, and the techno-nerd's world is made manifest. Photoshop then serves as the vehicle for image manipulation. The process is cyclical, with two designers working continually together, starting with a "kit" (models) and ending with a "kit" (images), with the idea becoming the thread that binds these vignettes together.

Purpose of the Drawing

An analytical drawing intended to be a summary of a project; a layered explanation of the techno-nerd's world. In the end, it is a diagrammatic, multidirectional map intended to motivate the viewer (as well as the designers) toward further discourse; not unlike the preface to a book, it is simply the beginning.

Design Concept

Programmatic pieces of two urban blocks are divided into dayclub/nightclub. The space of the nightclub is a completely visual and auditory environment created by a series of movable panels that are bombarded with liquid crystal displays. The character of the space can be completely changed simply by changing the set of images and the music. The dayclub is divided into two hypothetical user personalities, codenames techno-nerd and unabomber. The techno-nerd lives in an architecturally reconfigurable environment. The walls rotate to create various combinations of spaces specifically for Internet access, business functions, computer games, and so on. Sunlight enters the home/workplace of the techno-nerd only from the front and rear vertical walls. The home of the unabomber is an oasis from technological advances. These apartments are pure phenomena without television or computers. The roof of faceted glass accepts most of the light and the materials are highly textured.

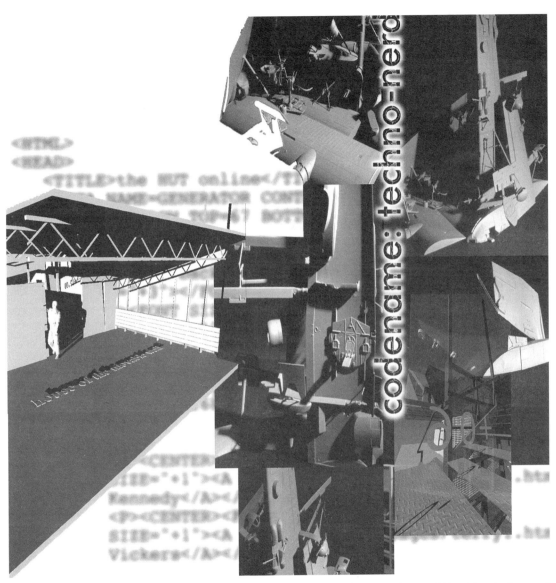

codename: techno-nerd (dayclub w.d. phase one)
Drawing: kevinkennedy/terryvickers

San Francisco, California

The Penthouse for a Playful King, San Francisco, California

Profile

Inglese Architecture is a dynamic young firm dedicated to the creation of fine residential, commercial, and civic architecture. Mark English and associates Jeff Gard and Star Jennings follow a team-leader approach to design, in which talented sculptors, artisans, and builders are involved as collaborators from the beginning of the design process through the completion of construction. In the studio, the same collaborative approach is found. Each studio member is encouraged to pursue design investigations in parallel with the others, resulting in an alloyed solution. Each project is specifically tailored to the needs and personality of the client. This process produces work with a variety of "styles," but with consistent attention to natural and artificial light effects, color, and material explorations. In essence, the architects perceive the final built project as an artifact—an object shaped by the parameters of client, culture, environment, technology, and finance. The computer modeling/drafting program Archicad by Grahisoft is used extensively for three-dimensional fixed and animated building studies, as well as for the final production drawings. Handmade models and drawings are used to complement the computer work.

Explanation of the Drawing Process and Technique

Detailed computer model views of the building are made within the Archicad program and saved as TIFF files. Selected background views are scanned into the computer as Adobe Photoshop images, and altered in size, shape, and opacity. The background images are provided to indicate the actual views available to the visitor. The final drawing is composed in Photoshop by layering the altered images together and trimming the perspective building images.

Purpose of the Drawing

The main purpose of the drawing is to collect the meaningful parameters that were used in the design of the project, as well as the resultant formal and spacial qualities. The audience is both the client and the studio team.

Design Concept

The architects believe that each design project is an artifact shaped by many parameters. The space within the penthouse is dominated by a strong horizontal vista dominated by larger-than-life landmarks: the Golden Gate Bridge, the Bay Bridge, Alcatraz, and Angel Island. The interior elements reflect a similar boldness in distinctive shape and material.

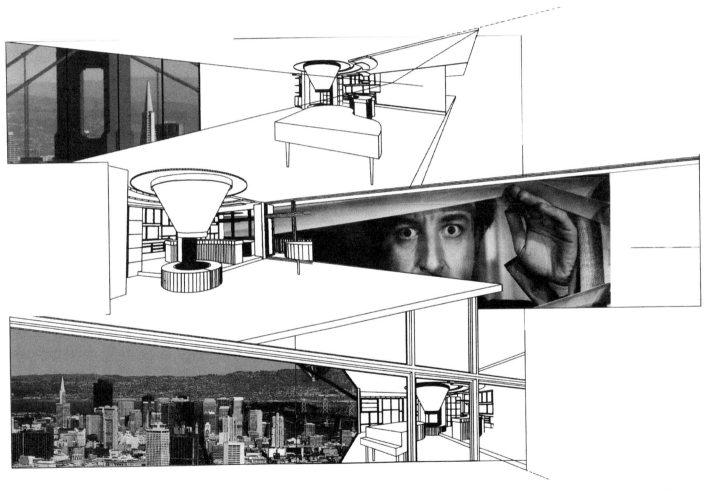

The Penthouse for a Playful King, San Francisco, California.
Design and drawing: Mark English, Jeff Gard, Star Jennings

Helmut Jahn

Murphy/Jahn Architects, Chicago, Illinois

State of Illinois Center, Chicago, Illinois

Profile

Helmut Jahn, president of Murphy/Jahn Architects, has earned a reputation on the cutting edge of progressive architecture. Under his guidance, the Murphy/Jahn practice has grown steadily, and has succeeded in combining the best of design creativity and corporate professionalism. Murphy/Jahn maintains a diversified practice, serving a broad spectrum of private, corporate, and governmental clients. The diversity of work stimulates a cross-fertilization of ideas and an intellectual freshness derived from addressing and resolving new architectural challanges. The Murphy/Jahn approach to design is both rational and intuitive: to strive to give each building its own philosophical and intellectual identity.

Explanation of the Drawing Process and Technique

Site/building plan and section enclosing central atrium; Prismacolor pencil on textured rendering paper.

Purpose of the Drawing

The purpose of the drawing is to convey a sense of the three-dimensional space that is created with the central rotunda and interaction with the surrounding office space.

Design Concept

The unusual form of this state office building is a fusion of images: traditional ones from classical courthouses and capitols and contemporary images of a government building that seems accessible and inviting. The rounded facade and the immense public space within—a circular skylit atrium rising the full height of the building and thrusting through the roof—are intended to recall the forms and embody the monumentality of traditional rotundas and domes.

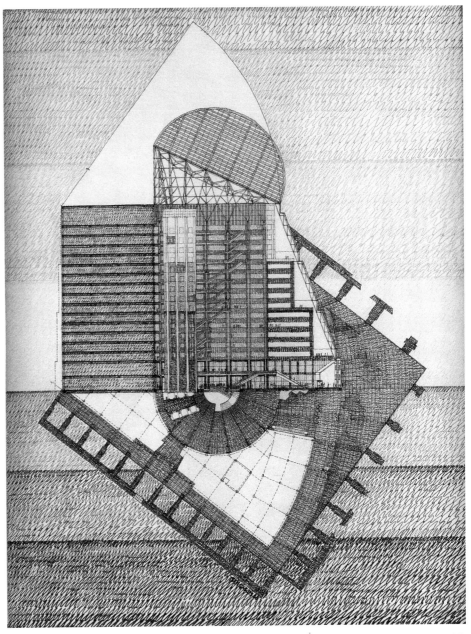

State of Illinois Center, Chicago, Illinois. See Color Plate 28.
Drawing: Helmut Jahn

Helmut Jahn

Murphy/Jahn Architects, Chicago, Illinois

Constantini Museum

Explanation of the Drawing Process and Technique

Computer-generated three-dimensional interior model using Microstation Masterpiece. Image retouched in Adobe Photoshop and formatted for printing in Adobe Pagemaker. Iris print, 20"×30" in size.

Purpose of the Drawing

To understand the interior space created for the museum and gallery with flexibility of space and use of daylight.

Design Concept

The Constantini Museum is a flexible venue for exhibits and gatherings. Exterior and interior conditions modulate its appearance. Within a minimalist attitude, these dynamics of change make the museum a flexible tool and give it much complexity and interest. The design of the museum is about light. Around trays of two concrete slabs, containing the cellular fixed functions and all services, a light steel and glass structure encloses the permanent and temporary exhibition areas.

Constantini Museum.
Drawing: Helmut Jahn with T. J. McLeish

Helmut Jahn

Murphy/Jahn Architects, Chicago, Illinois

Sony Center Berlin, Berlin, Germany

Explanation of the Drawing Process and Technique

Collage; four-color lithograph. Original sketches in pen and colored ink with site plan and elevation layer on top.

Purpose of the Drawing

A poster showing the progress of the Sony project in Berlin, illustrating the development of plan, facades, and study details.

Design Concept

Propelling Berlin into the 21st century, the Sony Center's Passage and Forum introduce bold new concepts in urban open space. Beyond the urban, architectural, and space concepts, it is the mix of uses that assures true urban life and activity in the Sony Center. It becomes a new type of urban interaction among working, living, shopping, entertainment, and relaxation.

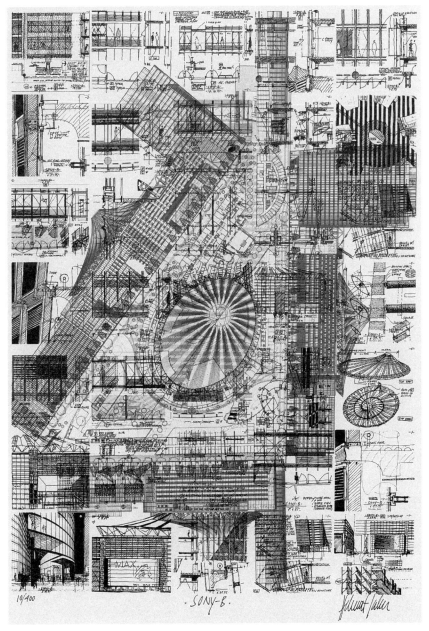

Sony Center Berlin, Berlin, Germany. See Color Plate 29.
Drawing: Helmut Jahn

Helmut Jahn

Murphy/Jahn Architects, Chicago, Illinois

Northwestern Atrium Center, Chicago, Illinois

Explanation of the Drawing Process and Technique

Airbrush on KP-5 high-contrast photographic paper with printed line drawing.

Purpose of the Drawing

To illustrate the interaction of the train station and atriums at the lower level of the building with the office tower above. The introduction of light coordinates references of train traffic with the facade of the building.

Design Concept

The Northwestern Terminal Project is a combined commuter terminal and office building complex, replacing the existing Chicago and Northwestern Train Station. The building forms a major "gateway" from the station to Madison Street, which acts as a major connector to the Loop to the east and the urban renewal area to the west. It thus removes the imposing "Chinese wall" effect the existing station had toward the growth of the Central Business District toward the west.

Northwestern Atrium Center, Chicago, Illinois. See Color Plate 30.
Drawing: Helmut Jahn with T. J. McLeish

Keelan P. Kaiser

Adjunct Faculty, University of Nebraska-Lincoln; common DIVERGENCE, Lincoln, Nebraska

A Center for the Study of Television and Film (Academic Project)

Profile

Keelan P. Kaiser directs **common** DIVERGENCE, a design studio dedicated to the execution of ambitious, spirited, and unique ideas emphasizing material beauty and visual contrast. The studio engages in architecture, graphic design, and furniture design. In addition, Mr. Kaiser is a visiting assistant professor in the College of Fine and Performing Arts, University of Nebraska-Lincoln, teaching foundation design and graphic design. He previously served on the adjunct faculty of the College of Architecture, University of Nebraska-Lincoln. His practice experience includes work at Eisenman Architects.

Explanation of the Drawing Process and Technique

Three-dimensional model generated in AT&T Topas, plotted in AutoCAD R13. Color wire frame is plotted on 30"×40" bond paper, with airbrush paint to identify floor planes through gallery modules.

Purpose of the Drawing

The aerial wire frame drawing communicates the volumes of the gallery modules. The volumes imply motion and movement within their general physical proximities. The interior wire frame drawing allows a visibility "through" the modules by using the transparency of the wire frame. This visual flexibility is useful in communicating the modulation and formal implications of movement.

Design Concept

The project studied the use of a computer modeling program as a tool during the formative stages of design. The computer modeling, much like schematic chipboard modeling, was used as a volume fabricator and manipulator. The formal strategy is intended to express a series of four objects simultaneously occupying subtly different locations.

A Center for the Study of Television and Film (Academic Project). See Color Plate 31.
Design, drawing, and photography: Keelan P. Kaiser

Keelan P. Kaiser

Adjunct Faculty, University of Nebraska-Lincoln; common DIVERGENCE, Lincoln, Nebraska

Claflin Work/Live Studios (*An adaptive reuse project in an old printing company warehouse in Lincoln, Nebraska*)

Explanation of the Drawing Process and Technique

Graphite on 20″×30″ vellum paper. The drawing is produced in two parts: First, the overall space and objects within the space are laid out in light pencil. Tonal values are applied to the surface. Several layers of graphite dusting are applied, with each layer secured to the surface with spray fixative. As the image becomes built up, the depth and volume of the drawing increase. Last, the objects in the environment are drawn in hard line to sharpen the edges of the spatial wire frame.

Purpose of the Drawing

The objective of these drawings is to study how the dividing systems, both in hard and soft materials, affect the open character of the primary volume. The wire frame nature of the drawing allows visualizing the entire space, the intermediate space, and shallow spaces simultaneously. This affects the overall perception and sensations of locating oneself within the environment.

Design Concept

The objective of the design was to maintain the integrity of a concrete and plaster work center, previously a printing company and now a design company/residence. With limited permanent intrusion and multiple temporary and flexible dividing canvas systems, the spaces maintain the openness of the work house while allowing the subtle divisions between working and living spaces. The living spaces are more semiopaque and closed, becoming more translucent and open as one approaches the working spaces.

Claflin Work/Live Studios. See Color Plate 32.
Design: Keelan P. Kaiser, Thomas Gallagher
Drawing: Matt Stoffel
Photography: Keelan P. Kaiser

Kajima Corporation

Tokyo, Japan

Office Building, Tokyo, Japan

Profile

Twenty years after its establishment in 1840, Kajima Corporation constructed Japan's first Western-style building—the Eiichibankan—in Yokohama. Since then, Kajima has rapidly developed its operations by anticipating future trends in all types of construction-related needs. The company's activities have encompassed the railway construction and electric power development that propelled Japan's initial modernization, as well as the coastal industrial developments, high-rise structures, nuclear power plants, and maritime-related projects that helped the nation rise quickly to economic superpower status. Today, as one of Japan's leading construction companies, Kajima maintains subsidiaries in North America, Europe, and Asia and is active in construction and real estate development businesses around the world. With an eye to the dynamic changes under way in the operating and social environments, Kajima will continue to evolve, supported by superior technological expertise, rich human resources, and a pioneer spirit.

Explanation of the Drawing Process and Technique

Computer-generated line drawings with a rendered perspective view. Early in the design process, the sheet was composed on CATIA, which consists of various "windows" opening up onto the three-dimensional model. Design proceeded from a blank screen and consisted of manipulating and analyzing CATIA solids. Each time a variation of the design was finalized, this sheet was produced autometically from the three-dimensional model. In some variations, parts of the building protruding beyond the set "windows" required slight adjustments, especially in the sequences at the bottom of the sheet. The three-dimensional solid model was produced on CATIA during the design process. Rendering was completed on in-house "REALS" ray tracing software. Drawings printed out in electrostatic plotter Output format include digitally produced print, slide, and 4"×5" positive.

Purpose of the Drawing

Various computer-generated drawings composed together for the purpose of design study.

Design Concept

Floors two through four function as a library, with offices on floors five through seven. The front of the building responds to the street with conventional curtain-wall construction, while the entire rear facade becomes a truss wall containing core elements: elevators, exterior stairways, restroom modules, and exposed mechanical equipment. Angular study nooks protrude through the truss wall on the library floors.

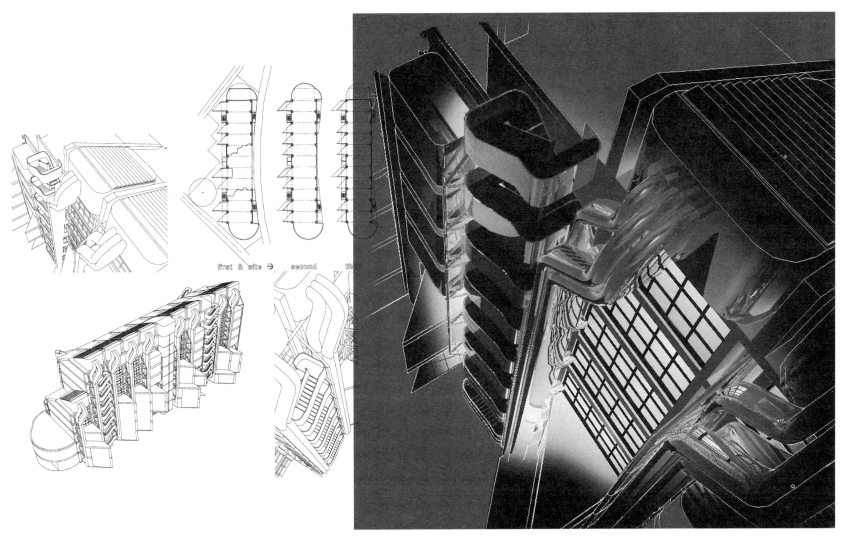

Office Building, Tokyo, Japan. See Color Plate 33.
Design: A. Scott Howe and Tomohito Okudaira for Kajima Corporation
Rendering: A. Scott Howe

Kajima Corporation

Tokyo, Japan

Memorial Hall Project, Kushiro, Japan

Explanation of the Drawing Process and Technique

Computer graphics composite image. Three-dimensional solid model was produced on CATIA during the design process. Rendering was completed on inhouse "REALS" ray tracing software. Photomontage by Shimatronix graphics paint system. Output format includes digitally produced print, slide, and 4"×5" positive. Presentation panel for competition, 2048×1360 pixels.

Purpose of the Drawing

Although many images and wire frames were produced as design aids during the design process, this panel image was put together for the final presentation. Several images and drawings produced during the design stage were employed as elements in the final image.

Design Concept

Established at a ruin site within the city, the memorial becomes an amphitheater where the entire town is the stage, visible through clear screens containing liquid crystal cores. Visitors can relax on the tiered circular seating with their backs to the center and observe the actual town or images of the past overlaid on those of the present. "Media towers" laid out in a grid pattern on the site and extending into the town have multiple functions of recording and playback of sound and images, image projection, hologram projection, weather data recording, and the like.

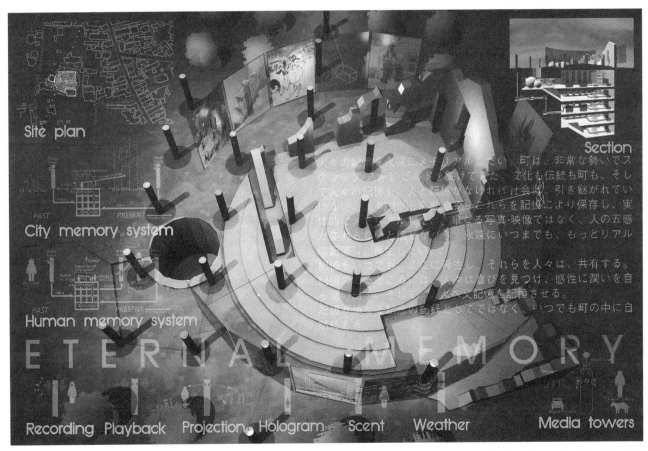

Site plan

City memory system

Human memory system

PAST PRESENT

PAST PRESENT

ETERNAL MEMORY

Section

Recording Playback Projection Hologram Scent Weather Media towers

人々の記憶を永遠にメモリアルしたい 町は、非常な勢いでス
クラップ・アンドに を続けてきた。文化も伝統も町も、そし
て人々の記憶も、人 記憶がなければ社会 引き継がれてい
けない。 物 釜これらを記憶により保存し、実
的に 、単なる写真・映像ではなく、人の五感
 ながら、永遠にいつまでも、もっとリアル
 に再生し、それらを人々は、共有する。
人々は喜びを見つけ、感性に潤いを自
 々、人記憶を記憶させる。
記 の記録としてではなく、いつでも町の中に自

Memorial Hall Project, Kushiro, Japan. See Color Plate 34.
Design: A. Scott Howe and Yuji Kaido for Kajima Corporation
Rendering: Chizuko Sami

Kajima Corporation

Tokyo, Japan

PAVILION Project, Tokyo, Japan

Explanation of the Drawing Process and Technique

Computer graphics perspective rendering, 1100 mm × 600 mm. Wire frame perspective of three-dimensional solid model produced on CATIA was Xeroxed and masked, and background paint applied with a roller. Remaining detail was applied with watercolor and acrylic.

Purpose of the Drawing

Drawing was produced for final presentation purposes.

Design Concept

A sphere consisting of a double-walled truss structure suspended away from the ground. All structural and mechanical members are completely integrated in an easy-to-assemble kit of parts. Interior spaces include a domed theater, waiting areas, exhibit spaces, and the like. Energy generation towers are placed in a grid on the site and include windmills, hydroelectric generation, and solar panels, which double as shading structures for an exterior amphitheater / waiting area.

PAVILION project, Tokyo, Japan. See Color Plate 35.
Architectural design: A. Scott Howe and Hiroshi Ono for Kajima Corporation
Rendering: Go Nishiyama

Peter Kommers

School of Architecture, Montana State University, Bozeman, Montana

Five Small Rooms—Spring 1996 (*Room 302-C, Hotel Toledano-on-the-Ramblas, Barcelona*)

Profile

Peter Kommers teaches architectural design at Montana State University's School of Architecture and maintains an architectural practice and painting studio. His architectural design studio emphasizes drawing as a fundamental internalization of architecture's powers. Mr. Kommers draws and paints in pursuit of inclusive images based on multiple readings of sites animated by the spirit of human circumstance and place.

Explanation of the Drawing Process and Technique

A very small amount of light pencil drawing began the initial fragment of the sunlit elevation. It was then committed to watercolor using a value-delineated approach. Line drawings for the remaining plan images were completed in ink and finishing washes were added after the line work. The wall image is a borrowed and pasted stamp.

Purpose of the Drawing

The brilliantly sunlit stuccoed surface across a light well from the hotel room seemed to bounce the sounds of a barking dog, along with the sensations of a beckoning city, entirely through the tiny space. The purpose was to examine the promise of city forays to come with the thrill of this well-lighted place.

Design Concept

The concept for this piece was first inspired by brilliant Catalonian light reflected into the room and expressed in an elevational one-point perspective. This was combined with references to interior room plan, interior elevation, and paraline without disturbing the feasibility of these differing views working together to create a full sense of layered impressions.

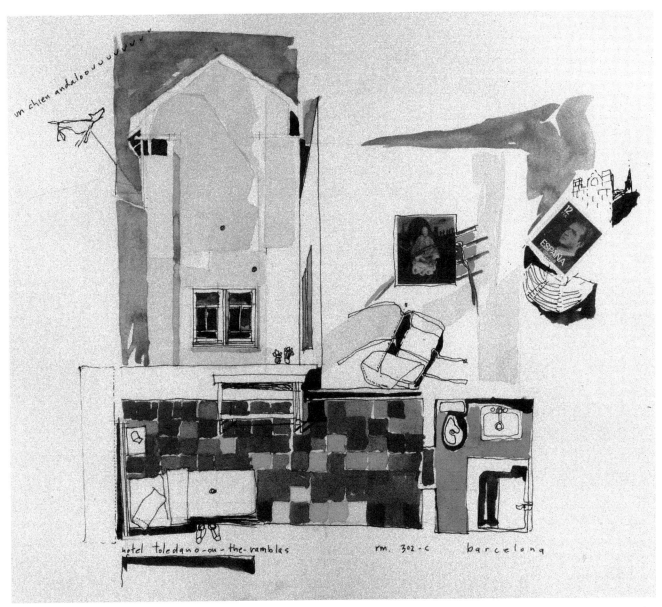

Room 302-C, Hotel Toledano-on-the-Ramblas, Barcelona. See Color Plate 36.
Drawing: Peter Kommers

Sandra Davis Lakeman (with Elizabeth Grossman)

Professor of Architecture, California Polytechnic State University, San Luis Obispo, California

San Marco Orphanage, Siena, Italy

Profile

Sandra Davis Lakeman is a registered architect in Oregon and a professor of architecture at California Polytechnic State University. Her photographs are represented by William Joseph Gallery, Portland, Oregon. Her work titled *Natural Light and the Italian Piazza* has been in major exhibitions in Italy and in the offices of the American Institute of Architects in Portland, Oregon. Sponsors have been the Graham Foundation for Advanced Studies in the Fine Arts, L. J. Skaggs and Mary C. Skaggs Foundation, the National Endowment for the Arts, Banca Toscana, Cal Poly, and the Comune di Siena. Her exhibition catalogue with the same title is distributed in the United States by the University of Washington Press, Seattle, and in Europe by Gingko Press, Hamburg, Germany.

Explanation of the Drawing Process and Technique

A loose scribble technique of colored pencil on white Canson board gracefully combines the building and site plans with the major streetside and countryside elevations. The drawing was part of a series of three coordinated boards, which delineated a revitalized Social Services building near Porta San Marco, the southwestern gateway of Siena. This drawing was influenced by the work of San Francisco landscape architect and graphic designer Barbara Stauffacher Solomon.

Purpose of the Drawing

The work was produced in a Cal Poly civic architecture design studio and shown as part of a student exhibition in the Palazzo Patrizi for the Comune di Siena, Italy.

Design Concept

Although this project was a student's hypothetical project when proposed, the actual Social Services *recupero* of the defunct San Marco Orphanage has now become a reality, renamed Unitá Minime Intervento, a unified minimal intervention. Ten different societal functions, from a daytime nursery for the young to a dormitory for college-aged youth to a day hospital for senior citizens, as well as four levels of underground parking, are implementations of the new Bernardo Secchi Master Plan of Siena, as well as Elizabeth Grossman's project concept.

SOCIAL SERVICES

San Marco Orphanage, Siena, Italy. See Color Plate 37.
Drawing: Elizabeth Grossman

Logic Error

Minneapolis, Los Angeles, Seattle

Faktura—Earth

Profile

Founded in 1990, Logic Error is a collective of designers engaged in the art of architectural investigation using computer modeling, rendering, and animation: "We explore our designs through the virtual dimension in the hope of better understanding the world around us. The TV and movie culture of the day, as well as theatrical production, influences us. We take the traditions of architecture one step further, adding time and movement to the process. Our hope is to lead you through an exhilarating spatial experience that leaves one to question and think about the future." The work is experimental, a moving collage of spontaneous visceral emotion. It engages sign, symbol, and myth. Animations portray theoretical constructions played out against a landscape of various architectural solutions from projects both real and ephemeral—taking the position that it is possible to be in two places at one time.

Explanation of the Drawing Process and Technique

The image has its origins in computer modeling. Cyber workstations were created in AES (Architectural Engineering Series), a 3D modeling software developed by IBM in the mid-eighties. The models were exported into 3Dstudio, material mapped, and rendered. Flight paths were set up in the keyframer window to create computer animation. Multiple stills from the animation were brought into photoshop and collaged.

Purpose of the Drawing

The composition was created for artistic purposes. It showcases Faktura, a particular segment of an ongoing discovery process that seeks to analyze our surroundings and communicate ideas through a highly technical medium.

Design Concept

The genesis of the Faktura comes from a security control center designed for the purpose of "watching and controlling" from a singular position. This node or teleman, allows one to be able to communicate with various aspects of the built environment. It represents data streams of logic and error—transferred through time, studied, and transferred again through a random, yet patterned organization of information "keyholes." These streams are then mapped with regularity onto a synoptic transfer cell or brain. The resulting cities of information represent a control point of data collection and transfer similar to that of the internet.

Faktura—Earth. See Color Plate 38.
Digital Drawing: Logic Error

Designers:
Derek Robert McCallum, Glasgow School of Arts, Scotland
Chris Mullen, Sci-arc
David Eric Koenen, University of Minnesota
Joey Myers, North Dakota State University
Paul Quinn Davis, University of Minnesota
Michael Hnastchenko, University of Minnesota

Associate Professor, School of Architecture, University of Southwestern Louisiana, Lafayette, Louisiana

Cylindrical House "Calderara," Emperia, Italy

Profile

George S. Loli studied architecture in Florence, Italy, and worked with Paolo Riani and Andrea Bertacca. Currently, he is an associate professor of architecture at the University of Southwestern Louisiana, Lafayette, Louisiana. He teaches design, product design, and graphic communication at various levels of the bachelor's degree program. Exploring the use of a variety of color media in sketches is his particular interest. His work in watercolor can be seen in a number of publications from Europe and traveling exhibits in Paris.

Explanation of the Drawing Process and Technique

The drawing is a hybrid elevation/section/plan with a distinguishable context offering a sense of place. It started as a mechanically drawn study and concluded with the spontaneous mark of the hand, along with lead and color pencil. The use of a square format is a reflection of the symmetry between the part exposed and the one buried into the hillside.

Purpose of the Drawing

The drawing explores the architectural possibilities of an extreme site condition with the clarity of an aboveground elevation and a sectional hint of a wine cellar buried into the slope of the hill. Compatibility with indigenous natural elements was a concern, as was the consistency between the main structure and an extremely visible light beacon at the top of the hill. An early sketch of the design was done to facilitate studies of plan and elevation simultaneously. The drawing is a process sketch, not intended for precise information transfer.

Design Concept

The drawing is a fantastical dialogue between a radically sloped hillside and a tower-type architectural intervention. The project is for a terraced vineyard beneath the Italian village of Calderara-Imperia to house a wine connoisseur and his elaborate collection of fine liquid spirits.

PIANTA

G. Loli

Cylindrical House "Calderara," Emperia, Italy.
See Color Plate 39.
Drawing: George S. Loli

George S. Loli

Associate Professor, School of Architecture, University of Southwestern Louisiana, Lafayette, Louisiana

Villa a Scandicci, Florence, Italy

Explanation of the Drawing Process and Technique

The design sketch is a collection of fragments comprising part of a much larger complex. It is primarily a technical elevation, executed on the drawing board in pencil and then elaborated in terms of form and light with freehand application of lead pencil, colored pencil, and splashes of watercolor. There is also the hint of a planometric projection superimposed across the sky. The drawing was done on 50/50 cotton/linen paper with a vertical texture to enhance the expression of concrete formwork.

Purpose of the Drawing

The drawing is one of many design sketches exploring the sculptural massing of elements in the light of "cast-in-place" concrete. Several elevation studies were done to study the possibilities of sculpted space by rendering deep shadows reflecting the absence of light on concrete planes. The primary use of lead pencil was an opportunity to explore the monochromatic tonal quality of concrete.

Design Concept

The original client for the villa was a sculptor by trade and was looking for a sculpted environment in which to live and work. Multiple terraces invited a memory of Carrera, from which the sculptor quarried his stone. The landscaping is an expression of randomly arranged material remnants from the sculptor's studio.

TERRAZZA

Villa a Scandicci, Florence, Italy. See Color Plate 40.
Drawing: George S. Loli

Lubowicki/Lanier Architects

El Segundo, California

O'Neill Guesthouse, Brentwood, California

Profile

The architectural firm of Lubowicki/Lanier was founded by Paul Lubowicki and Susan Lanier in 1988 and is considered to be one of the up-and-coming young firms in Los Angeles. Mr. Lubowicki and Ms. Lanier have designed several residential and commercial projects, fabricated numerous furniture pieces (some of which have been exhibited locally), and lectured at various architectural institutions. Both Mr. Lubowicki and Ms. Lanier have taught as visiting faculty members at a number of institutions, including Harvard University Graduate School of Design, University of Texas at Arlington School of Architecture, and Southern California Institute of Architecture. Mr. Lubowicki's and Ms. Lanier's approach to design considers each project as a unique opportunity to bring together the program, site, client, context, and user into a coherent set of relationships at both architectural and human scales. It is through the combination of these relationships that the character and uniqueness of each project reveals itself in the building.

Explanation of the Drawing Process and Technique

Site plan with longitudinal section and cross-section. These drawings are based on the Krazy Kat comics by George Herriman, and are meant to evoke the Sunday comics. The process started with an original ink and zip-a-tone color drawing, which was scanned and printed on computer by Nash Editions. The background drawings are silkscreen cartoon images on a handmade paper over which was silkscreened a swath of clear coat, creating a frame onto which the computer image was printed. Additional drawings were scanned and rearranged onto the paper, making this an additive process that can continue to evolve.

Purpose of the Drawing

The O'Neill Guesthouse drawings and model were generated for an exhibition titled "Angels and Franciscans—Innovative Architecture from Los Angeles and San Francisco" at the Leo Castelli/Gagosian Gallery in New York, which exhibited the work of 15 architects from Los Angeles and San Francisco.

Design Concept

The architectural language is based on the associative meaning derived through the juxtaposition of symbolic elements. Similar elements were designed to express dissimilar qualities. Dissimilar elements were designed to express "related" qualities. They coexist to intensify the various aspects of the interior and exterior (i.e., can one experience being within the garden and within an architectural enclosure at the same time?). One's experience of the site extends this dialogue further by addressing two worlds simultaneously: the neighborhood/street and the garden. Both worlds are composed of similar elements. The world belonging to the neighborhood/street consists of a front yard, the existing house, and a rear garden deck bordered by a pool. It is joined by a bridge over the pool to the world of the garden: the guesthouse, a lower garden, and a creek.

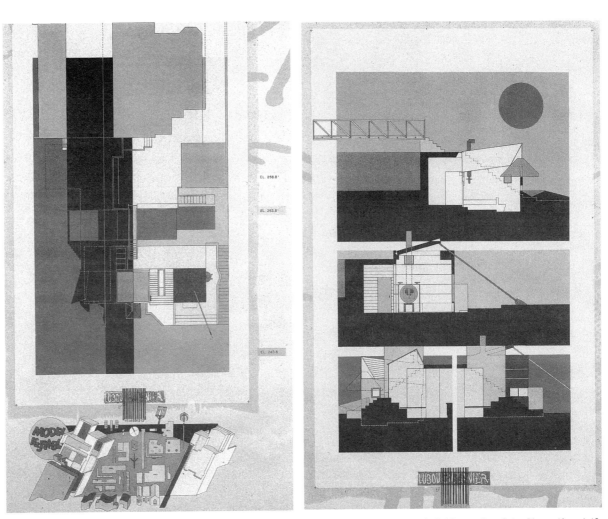

O'Neill Guesthouse, Brentwood, California. See Color Plates 41 and 42.
Design and drawing: Susan Lanier and Paul Lubowicki

Adjunct Professor, School of Architecture, Montana State University, Bozeman, Montana

"Virtual to Actual Memorial," a Competition Design Proposal

Profile

William E. Massie, a graduate of Columbia University Graduate School of Architecture and holder of a BFA from Parsons School of Design, was an adjunct faculty member from 1994 to 1996 at Columbia University; he now teaches at Montana State University. His independent work consists primarily of theoretical and built projects that function in and out of the virtual world of the computer.

Explanation of the Drawing Process and Technique

The relief drawing/model was constructed by a combination of two- and three-dimensional computer drawings. Several layers were designed and constructed exclusively in digital form. They were then used to write "tool paths" in "Mastercam" software. The tool paths were then used as the "code" to computerize the drawing with the use of a computer-controlled milling machine. The C.N.C. milling machine subtracted the prescribed material and the drawing, in a sense, was revealed. The board material is a white, monolithic plastic.

Purpose of the Drawing

The drawings were submitted to a 1997 design competition for a memorial at the site of the Battle of Little Bighorn.

Design Concept

The hybrid drawings were produced for the competition to prove that if this project was chosen to be built, the same computer files that made the competition boards could theoretically be used to build the actual memorial. The scale of the computer drawings would be changed and a larger computer-controlled milling machine would be used to fabricate the memorial out of concrete.

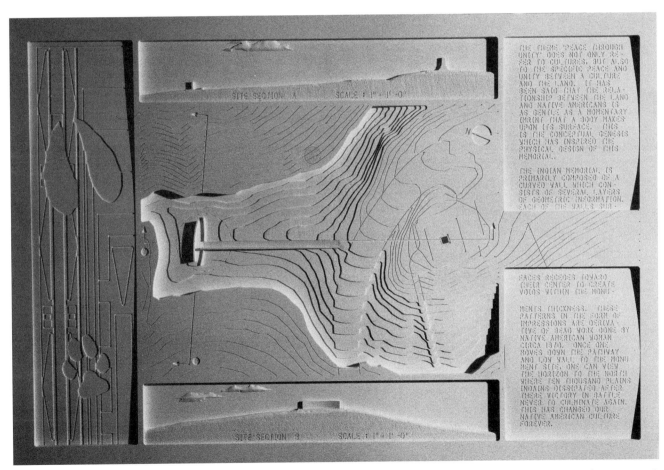

"Virtual to Actual Memorial," a competition design proposal.
Computer-etched drawing/model: William E. Massie

David Thomas Mayernik

Florence, Italy and Allentown, Pennsylvania

Project for the Via della Conciliazione, Rome

Profile

David Thomas Mayernik is an urban designer, architect, and fresco painter who has been named one of the top 40 architects in the United States under age 40. He is a fellow of the American Academy in Rome and is the winner of several competitions (including the Competition for the Completion of the Saint Paul Capitol Grounds, with partner Thomas Norman Rajkovich). He is currently developing the master plan and several new buildings for the campus of the American School in Switzerland.

Explanation of the Drawing Process and Technique

Pencil and watercolor on Arches cold press watercolor paper. 30"×40".

Purpose of the Drawing

An analytical drawing that combines both layered and assembled compositional strategies. It creates an illusion of the real while acknowledging itself as an image on paper.

Design Concept

This analytical drawing documents the project to reinvent the Spina, or spine of buildings, destroyed in making Mussolini's Via della Conciliazione, and reinvesting the approach to Saint Peter's with a meaningful and ennobling allegorical procession. The drawing documents the Borgo area plan, overlaid with a window surround from one of the proposed buildings, with a sketch at its feet of a design for a new gateway to Piazza San Pietro. In the upper right-hand corner, Piranesi's map of the Ager Vaticanus peers out, a reminder of the tradition of idealized planning in this area.

Project for the Via della Conciliazione, Rome. See Color Plate 43.
Drawing: David Thomas Mayernik

Morphosis

Santa Monica, California

Sun Tower, Seoul, Korea

Profile

Morphosis is a Santa Monica-based firm founded by Thom Mayne with the aspiration to build and design work of humanity, intellectual rigor, and intuitive design intelligence. Since 1974, Morphosis has maintained its vision of the practice of architecture as a collective enterprise, with an interest in producing work with a meaning that can be understood by absorbing and comprehending the culture for which it was made. The firm's personnel resources consist of an experienced group of profesionals with a variety of backgrounds. The design innovations of Morphosis are consistently stimulated by the freedom that arises from a multitude of ideas, individual opinions, and academic dogma. At Morphosis, the design method has always been highly intuitive and reflexive. Morphosis strives to understand the arena of operation as one marked by contradiction, conflict, change, and dynamism. Its interests lie in producing work that contributes to the conversation, adding another strain to what some may hear as the cacophony of modern life. Morphosis' concern is to establish and work within coherencies or orders that are open-ended and multivalent, organizations that may require more than a cursory examination to discern.

Explanation of the Drawing Process and Technique

Digital collage. The folded-plane, "origami" characteristic of the screen wall element is a direct result of the use of the computer; the complex plane geometry of this structure could have been generated only using this technology.

Purpose of the Drawing

Conceptual study; folding study of the skin membrane.

Design Concept

The requirements for this tower included five floors of retail (including two basement floors) and penthouse offices for the international corporate headquarters of a clothing manufacturer. The architectural idea involved the separation of the formal demands of the surface from the pragmatic requirements of the body, which was a direct response to the requirements of economics as they confronted planning and zoning restrictions. The concept of "wrapping" is explored, along with the possibilities of producing forms that would define an architecture in isolation from the constraints of the body. Origami and garment pattern-making—the client designs and manufactures clothing—contributed to the manner in which the problem was solved. The volume of the building was enclosed with a "second skin" of perforated aluminum "fabric" set 20 cm away from the face of the concrete enclosure. This cloth-like membrane, freed of the pragmatic constraints of a typical building surface, responds in a more lyrical and abstract way to various forces. On the interior, it acts as a "brise-soleil," with the flexibility of adapting to different conditions of light on each facade.

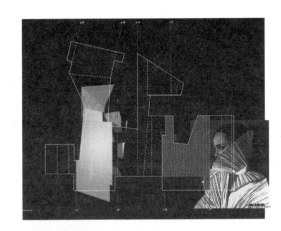
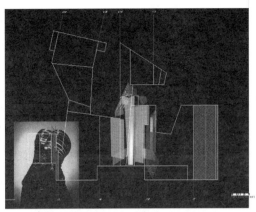
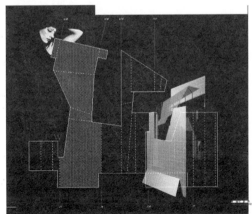
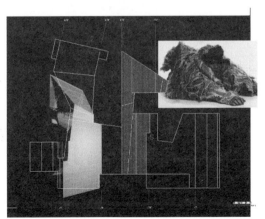

Sun Tower, Seoul, Korea.
Project manager: Eul Ho Suh
Project designers: Dave Grant, Kim Groves, Kristina Loock, Eui-Sung Yi
Project team: Min-Seok Baek, Jay Behr, Mark Briggs, Neil Crawford, Towan Kim, Richard Koschitz

Morphosis

Santa Monica, California

Arts Park Performing Arts Pavilion

Explanation of the Drawing Process and Technique

Montage, 32"×36".

Purpose of the Drawing

Presentation, exhibition, and publication.

Design Concept

This competition entry for the Performing Arts Pavilion Theatres at the Los Angeles Arts Park was focused primarily on the issue of how to juxtapose manmade objects with nature. In the design solution, articulated pieces of the structure are visible to passersby, configured to invite further exploration. The majesty and power of the arts go to a deeper level than what is outwardly apparent. The building, more than half buried, is revelatory in the sense that visible parts of the building are sculptural and kinetic in nature. Buildings set within a 200-acre parklike setting now become functional sculptures in keeping with the overall Arts Park concept.

Arts Park Performing Arts Pavilion. See Color Plate 44.
Design and drawing: Thom Mayne with Hans Boelling

Morphosis

Santa Monica, California

Seventy-Two Market Street, Venice, California

Explanation of the Drawing Process and Technique

Section and plan: superimposed plan below section drawing highlights structural supports and earthquake tension bars. Modeling paste and graphite on Mylar, 22"×33".

Purpose of the Drawing

Presentation, exhibition, and publication.

Design Concept

This restaurant is a new piece of construction, using a historic building on a small street in Venice, California, with a rich architectural heritage. Seventy-Two Market Street can be seen as a study in creativity and rebirth, exploring the dynamics of repressed aggression. The theme of the architectural intervention is a slightly rotated box within a rectangular volume. The canting of the box and access to it via a ramp inspire analogies to a womb and metaphors of rebirth. The project addresses issues of loss of center, destabilization, and the making and breaking of architecture.

Seventy-Two Market Street. See Color Plate 45.
Design and drawing: Thom Mayne with Kazu Arai

Eric Owen Moss

Eric Owen Moss Architects, Culver City, California

Pittard Sullivan Office Building, Culver City, California

Profile

Eric Owen Moss opened his office in 1973 in Los Angeles. Mr. Moss was educated at Berkeley and Harvard. He has recently held professorial chairs at Yale and Harvard, and appointments in Copenhagen and Vienna, in addition to Sci-Arc, where he began teaching in 1973 and is currently a member of the board of directors. His work has recently been exhibited in Duren, Germany; Barcelona, Spain; Tokyo, Japan; Lisbon, Portugal; and Copenhagen, Denmark; and he was one of the four American architects invited to represent the United States at the 1996 Venice Biennale. A Rizzoli monograph, *Eric Owen Moss: Buildings and Projects 2*, was published in 1995, along with *The Box*, published by Princeton Architectural Press in 1996, and *The Lawson/Westen House*, published by Phaeton Press in 1994. Upcoming books include *Gnostic Architecture*, a statement/manifesto of Moss' theory of design, to be published by Monacelli Press in 1998 and *PS* and *10 Years and the New City*, to be published by Images Press in 1998. Current projects include work in Vienna, Spain, France, New York, Los Angeles, and Culver City. Mr. Moss is the recipient of 34 design awards from Progressive Architecture and the American Institute of Architecture and is a fellow of the American Institute of Architecture.

Explanation of the Drawing Process and Technique

This drawing was a challenge to communicate the spatial qualities of the entry lobby of the Pittard Sullivan Office Building. The space is impossible to photograph in its entirety, so by stitching together multiple photos onto the background of a computer model, a hybrid was created between a photograph and a rendering that makes the geometry of the entire lobby intelligible.

Purpose of the Drawing

The purposes of this drawing are for presentation to the client, to exhibitions, and to publications. The hybrid images are made to provide a comprehensive understanding of the buildings from start to finish, from all angles. While they have an intrinsic beauty in themselves, their main function is to thoroughly inform.

Design Concept

The building acknowledges its past and the history of the area while moving decisively forward to create the landmark headquarters for a digital motion picture graphic design company. The ancillary buildings were removed from the site, except for a single brick wall and the double bowstring truss system. A four-story steel frame of wide flange beams and tube columns was built over the bowstrings, which now extend beyond the south wall and are exposed. A sequence of parallel walls follows the frames that follow the trusses: the south wall at the parking/building perimeter, a pair that enclose the double-loaded corridor, and a third that closes the office block. The building is enlarged by hooking four office blocks to the north wall.

Pittard Sullivan Office Building, Culver City, California.
Design: Eric Owen Moss
Drawing: Paul Groh

Eric Owen Moss Architects, Culver City, California

Samitaur Building, Los Angeles, California

Explanation of the Drawing Process and Technique

Computer-generated worm's-eye and bird's-eye perspectives.

Purpose of the Drawing

The purposes of this drawing are for presentation to the client, to exhibitions, and to publications. Although the initial project ideas are materialized in Mr. Moss' sketches, the projects change and develop over a long period. The composite drawings are a manifestation, a record, of the changes and amendments of the evolution of the project. The projects have a hybrid identity—traces of the project's original identity are evident in the end product, which, at first glance, may seem quiet different from its beginning.

Design Concept

Samitaur is the first substantial new office construction in the South-Central Los Angeles area since the 1992 riots. The building, a digital imaging company's new West Coast headquarters, is a two-story, 320-foot-long "air rights" office block, supported on steel legs that lift the block 16 feet over a pre-existing 30-foot-wide road. The position of the steel legs appear to be random, but the legs follow a simple logic. Columns are positioned so the existing on-grade buildings can continue to operate. The new legs fit between old roll-up doors, driveways, and windows.

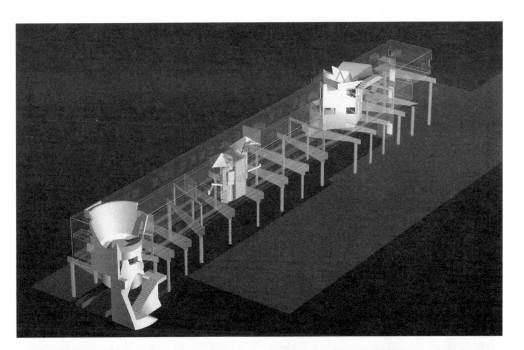

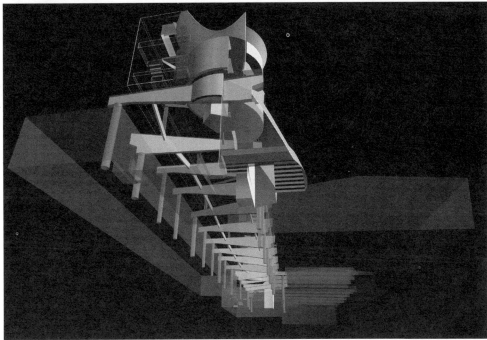

Samitaur Building, Los Angeles, California.
Design and Drawing: Eric Owen Moss
Drawing: Paul Groh

NBBJ Sports & Entertainment

Los Angeles, California

Staples Center—Home of the Los Angeles Lakers and Kings, Los Angeles, California

Profile

NBBJ Sports & Entertainment was created in 1995. Principals Michael Hallmark and Ron Turner were previously the founding principals of Ellerbe Becket Sports; they were joined at Ellerbe Becket in 1992 by design principal Dan Meis. After winning an international competition to design the $750 million Saitama Arena in Saitama, Japan, in 1995, the trio joined NBBJ to create a practice specializing in the design and integration of sports and entertainment facilities. Drawing on the unique resources and talent pool of Los Angeles, the practice has grown to include 90 architects and currently has numerous sports and entertainment facilities under construction in the United States, Europe, and Asia. Known for cutting-edge design and groundbreaking technology, NBBJ Sports & Entertainment is dedicated to elevating a building type rarely associated with world-class architecture.

Explanation of the Drawing Process and Technique

The process began with several loose, conceptual, freehand perspective sketches that illustrate the essence of the idea. Freehand drawings progressed quickly to computer studies in plan, section, and perspective simultaneously. Ultimately, the sketch became an ultrarealistic Silicon Graphics computer simulation illustrating color, texture, reflectivity, and transparency.

Purpose of the Drawing

This drawing composition is a layering of section, plan, and perspective in order to clearly demonstrate to the client the unmistakable interrelationship of form, plan, and section of this building type.

Design Concept

The intent of the design is to evoke motion, a dynamic quality inherent to the sports and entertainment events the building will host. The building is a disk "wrapped" by the entertainment components of the program. The form is intended to be evocative of a hockey puck moving swiftly across the ice.

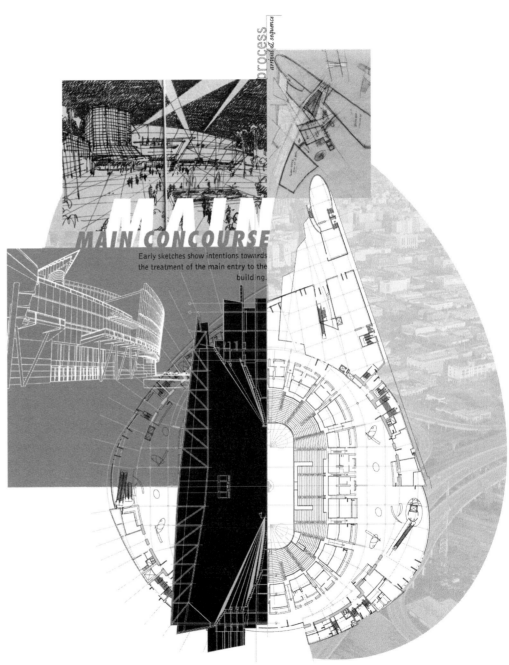

MAIN
MAIN CONCOURSE

Early sketches show intentions towards the treatment of the main entry to the building.

Staples Center—Home of the Los Angeles Lakers and Kings, Los Angeles, California. See Color Plate 46.
Design and Drawing: NBBJ Sports & Entertainment
Design principal: Dan Meis
Principal in charge: Michael Hallmark
Project manager: James Matson
Project architect: Vernon Pounds
Senior designer: Derek McCallum
Project team: Rania Alomar, Robert Dittes, Patrick Fejer, Fred Kim, Johee Kim, Olivia Ocampo, Heidi Painchaud, David Sweet, Todd Yamanouchi
Model and photography: John Lodge

NBBJ Sports & Entertainment

Los Angeles, California

Staples Center—Home of the Los Angeles Lakers and Kings, Los Angeles, California

Explanation of the Drawing Process and Technique

Same as for the image on the previous page.

Purpose of the Drawing

Same as for the image on the previous page.

Design Concept

Same as for the image on the previous page.

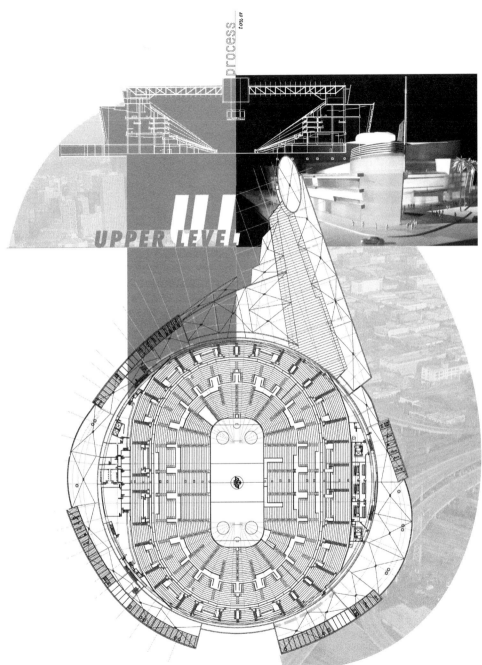

UPPER LEVEL III

process

Staples Center—Home of the Los Angeles Lakers and Kings, Los Angeles, California. See Color Plate 47.
Design and drawing: NBBJ Sports & Entertainment
Design principal: Dan Meis
Principal in charge: Michael Hallmark
Project manager: James Matson
Project architect: Vernon Pounds
Senior designer: Derek McCallum
Project team: Rania Alomar, Robert Dittes, Patrick Fejer, Fred Kim, Johee Kim, Olivia Ocampo, Heidi Painchaud, David Sweet, Todd Yamanouchi
Model and photography: John Lodge

Los Angeles, California

Paul Brown Stadium, Home of Cincinnati Bengals NFL Team, Cincinnati, Ohio

Explanation of the Drawing Process and Technique

Process sketches shown with final computer rendering. The process began with several loose, conceptual, freehand perspective sketches that illustrate the essence of the idea. Freehand drawings progressed quickly to computer studies in plan, section and perspective simultaneously. Ultimately, the sketch became an ultrarealistic Silicon Graphics computer simulation illustrating color, texture, reflectivity, and transparency.

Purpose of the Drawing

This design celebrates the relationship between the strength and mass of the structure and the lightness of the skin. This drawing is intended to "peel away" the layers of the building, exposing the skin, "organs," and "skeleton" of the building.

Design Concept

Long thought to be massive, cookie-cutter facilities with a "facade du jour," the intent of the design is to "break the mold" of NFL stadia. Sited on the Ohio riverfront, the building is fractured, opening the stadium to views of the city and the river. The dynamic quality of the building is exposed through translucent skins stretched taut over an intricate steel structure. The sense of lightness and movement is expressed through dramatic cantilevered seat decks and a translucent fabric canopy.

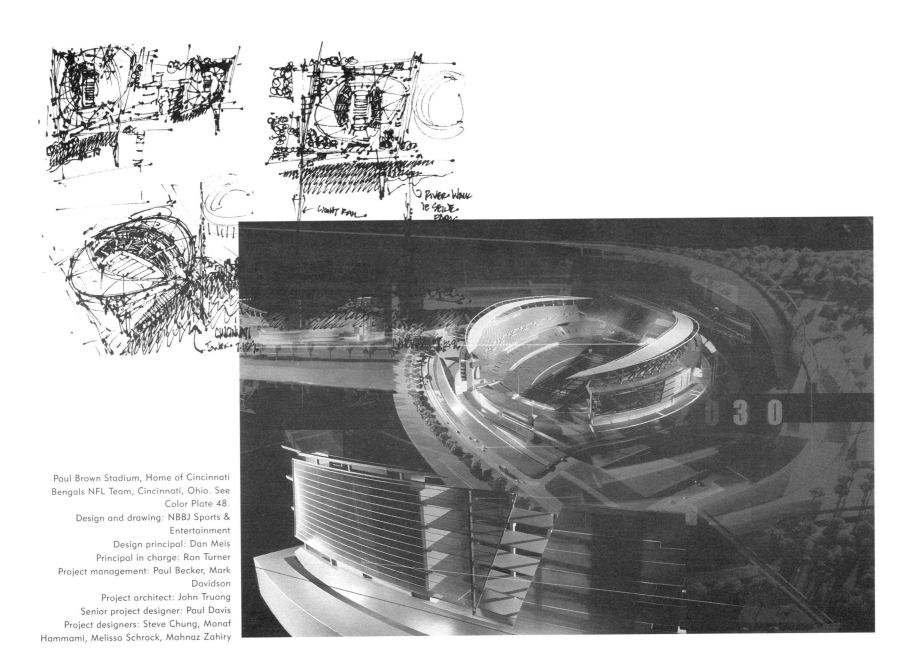

Paul Brown Stadium, Home of Cincinnati
Bengals NFL Team, Cincinnati, Ohio. See
Color Plate 48.
Design and drawing: NBBJ Sports &
Entertainment
Design principal: Dan Meis
Principal in charge: Ron Turner
Project management: Paul Becker, Mark
Davidson
Project architect: John Truong
Senior project designer: Paul Davis
Project designers: Steve Chung, Manaf
Hammami, Melissa Schrock, Mahnaz Zahiry

NBBJ Sports & Entertainment

Los Angeles, California

Paul Brown Stadium, Home of Cincinnati Bengals NFL Team, Cincinnati, Ohio

Explanation of the Drawing Process and Technique

Same as for the image on the previous page.

Design Concept

Same as for the image on the previous page.

Purpose of the Drawing

Same as for the image on the previous page.

Paul Brown Stadium, Home of Cincinnati Bengals NFL Team, Cincinnati, Ohio. See Color Plate 49.
Design and drawing: NBBJ Sports & Entertainment
Design principal: Dan Meis
Principal in charge: Ron Turner
Project management: Paul Becker, Mark Davidson
Project architect: John Truong
Senior project designer: Paul Davis
Project designers: Steve Chung, Manaf Hammami, Melissa Schrock, Mahnaz Zahiry

Alexis Pontvik Arkitekt, Stockholm, Sweden

Photographic Exhibition in the Nordic Museum, Stockholm, Sweden

Profile

Alexis Pontvik, Architect SAR/RIBA, was born in Stockholm in 1951. He was educated at the Academy of Arts in Düsseldorf, Germany, with Prof. H. Hollein and Prof. J. Stirling and at the Diploma School at the Architectural Association in London. He has had his own office since 1981, operating in a wide range of activities: town planning, landscape analysis, architectural design, exhibition design, and interior design. The city of Stockholm has been of special interest for the office over the last 15 years. A series of competitions, morphological analysis, and planning projects have been accomplished in recent years. Another frequent activity has been the collaboration with artists on a variety of projects.

Explanation of the Drawing Process and Technique

Drawn with ink on polyester film, 297 mm × 100 mm. A combination of a plan with a sketchy perspective. The plan illustrates the curving exhibition panels and the decreasing light toward the end, where a video film is shown. The light conditions are suggested by dotting the plan. The access to the exhibition and the scale in which the plan is drawn are integrated into the layout.

Purpose of the Drawing

Part of the intent of the drawing was to show variable lighting conditions of the spaces in the exhibit areas.

Design Concept

The existing space in the turn-of-the-century Nordic Museum in Stockholm is more than 54 meters long. The commission to design a photographic exhibition was resolved through a series of undulating panels, forming a rhythm in the center of the space. The plan illustrates the curving exhibition panels and the decreasing light toward the end, where a video film is shown. Part of the intent of the exhibition is to show a view of the city of Stockholm, which normally cannot be seen. The exhibition design provides a staircase that makes the view possible for visitors.

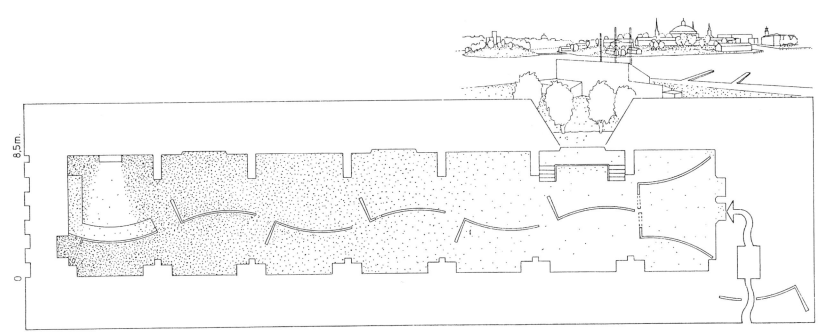

Photographic Exhibition in the Nordic Museum, Stockholm, Sweden.
Design and drawing: Alexis Pontvik Arkitekt

8,5 m.

0

Sheffield, England

Space-Form Analysis Schematic

Profile

The studio's primary concern is with structural aesthetics and refined detailing in architectural projects. As immortalized by Mies van der Rohe, the ethos of "God is in the details" forms an appropriate analogy to this young practice, which is still vying for recognition in a competitive industry. Ever keen to experiment and innovate, Studio-Z realizes the potential of the "cyber-era" and fully intends to exploit its potential, harnessed to the ever-progressive drive of technology and information. Dynamism is standard to this practice.

Explanation of the Drawing Process and Technique

An initial set of contextual site study drawings was produced, followed by a three-dimensional computer-rendered model. The original site plan was overlaid with greaseproof paper. A second translucent sheet was overlaid and heavy graphite lines were drawn over the primary frontages and profiles of the buildings in the region of the river. The primary lines of visual perception, or "vistas," were then linked to key points along the plan, where glimpses of certain buildings and contextually important objects could be identified and landmarked. The primary plane of each building that fronted onto the river was then progressively exploded perpendicularly away from the first in the direction of the river. Each new "force line" was effectively projected twice the distance away from the first one, in the same direction away from the baseline. The process was repeated for all further force lines and, in turn, for each side of the forms that could be seen facing the river. The intention was to articulate the notion that the farther one is away from an object, the less one is affected by its presence. The next stage of the process was to take the two-dimensional AutoCAD drawings and transform them into the three-dimensional virtual space of a computer, using 3D Studio Max. Using the original site plan as the basis, the drawing was digitized and then given depth by three-dimensional modeling. The model was then rendered, using plain and neutral colors for the general environment and the lofted three-dimensional shapes. The projected force planes were rendered using a type of frosted, semitranslucent glass. These, in turn, were given a luminescence that would highlight their presence and contextual effect.

Purpose of the Drawing

The drawing formed the basis of the generation of ideas for a built project located on the site. The process was carried out in order to produce a lucid and cogent spatial analysis of the site. It also served as a means of identifying crucial regions in the environment, contextual relationships, and the "warp and weft" inherent in the site. In the first instance, this involved the extrapolation of the site plan. The computerized model was generated in order to better understand this experiment and to give an architecturally realistic insight to the context. The contrast between the somewhat somber environment and the intense luminosity of the force planes allowed a much more visual exploration. Subtle coloration of each particular set of planes facilitated the analysis further. Hidden patterns could thus emerge and be read in parallel within the existing fabric. The planes added their own impact and electricity, with the intensity of each plane clearly articulated by the computer images.

Design Concept

This drawing, part of a series, was born out of an experimental analysis in which certain difficulties were evident in resolving the spatial relationships of the site layout. The drawings were hybrid not only in terms of technique, but also in terms of the approach and the inherent design development. The resultant process was both stimulating and unconventional, working beyond the orthodox principles of architectural drawing and innovating within the scope of the design processes.

Space-Form Analysis Schematic. See Color Plate 50.
Drawing: Zareen Mahfooz Rahman

Thomas Norman Rajkovich

Thomas Norman Rajkovich, Architect, Evanston, Illinois

Hortus Poeticus, Beverly Hills, California

Profile

The office of Thomas Norman Rajkovich, Architect, offers its clients unparalleled expertise in the design and execution of classical/traditional architecture and landscape. Mr. Rajkovich's work has been exhibited in Rome, Italy, Lisbon, Portugal, Beverly Hills, New York, Washington, D.C., Minneapolis, San Francisco, and Chicago. In 1986, in partnership with David T. Mayernik, he won the international competition for the design of the Minnesota State Capitol Grounds. The project covers 36 acres and is the largest proposed formal public garden of this century. Mr. Rajkovich's design for the Capitol Grounds earned him the Arthur Ross Award in Architecture from Classical America in 1987, as well as a Design Award from the American Society of Landscape Architects, Minnesota Chapter. He has been a visiting professor of architecture at the University of Notre Dame Rome Studies Program in Rome, Italy, the University of Notre Dame in South Bend, Indiana, the University of Illinois at Chicago, and the School of the Art Institute of Chicago. He has served as a guest design juror at the University of Notre Dame, the University of Illinois at Chicago, the School of the Art Institute of Chicago, the Cornell University Rome Program, the Rhode Island School of Design Rome Program, the Illinois Institute of Technology, and Andrews University. Mr. Rajkovich was recently named one of this decade's top 40 architects in the United States under the age of 40 by a distinguished panel of New York architects chaired by Robert A. M. Stern.

Explanation of the Drawing Process and Technique

Watercolor and ink wash are applied, in varying intensities and in multiple layers, to achieve a luminous transparency and saturated coloration over drafted pencil linework.

Purpose of the Drawing

Ideas, in the form of tectonic compositions and iconographic narratives, are best presented in drawings that are themselves narrative in nature. The plan of the Mansionus Musae pavilion, executed as a trompe l'oeil "drawing," is superimposed above its elevation. The differing degrees to which these two drawing types employ abstraction to achieve architectural representation suggested that the plan be represented as a "drawing," while the elevation is represented as a "view."

Design Concept

The Mansionus Musae, or "House of the Muses," is the principal element of the composition for the Hortus Poeticus. It serves simultaneously as a gateway to the park, an enclosure for three fountains with bronze representations of the nine Muses, and as a backdrop to the formal terrace, where musical and theatrical performances will occur.

Hortus Poeticus, Beverly Hills, California. See Color Plate 51.
Drawing: Thomas Norman Rajkovich

Resolution: 4 Architecture

New York, New York

Finkelstein Residence, New York

Profile

Founded in 1990, Resolution: 4 Architecture is a young office in New York consisting of partners Joseph Tanney and Robert Luntz and a small staff of talented and dedicated architects. Resolution: 4 is an architectural firm whose work probes deep into the latest developments in architectural design. Its decision to focus on "information" and "context" has led to an in-depth analysis of the main formal and technological languages of late modern culture. Resolution: 4 believes that the need for multiple readings and meanings exists, with a focus on the reanalysis, reinterpretation, and re-presentation of existing "essential information."

Explanation of the Drawing Process and Technique

The 6"×4" postcard composite is a composition produced in QuarkXPress on the Macintosh. Imported digitally, the partial first floor construction plan (30"×42") was produced in MiniCad on the Macintosh. The site plan is ink on Mylar (24"×36") with Zipatone, and was scanned. The model, made of Strathmore, chipboard, basswood, and cardboard, was photographed and scanned. On the front, the construction drawing serves as a background for the postcard, and the model photo serves as a background for the construction drawing.

Purpose of the Drawing

The composition was created specifically as a postcard intended for distribution to clients and colleagues.

Design Concept

Located in a rural landscape near the Hudson River, this house serves as an addition/renovation to an existing barn and its compound of 100-year-old structures. The pinwheeling Z part reinforces the existing formal vehicular entry court, while creating an informal viewing court off the back of the house. Each bar of the Z is articulated by its location in the landscape, accommodating views of Bear Mountain, meadows, woods, and a nearby pond.

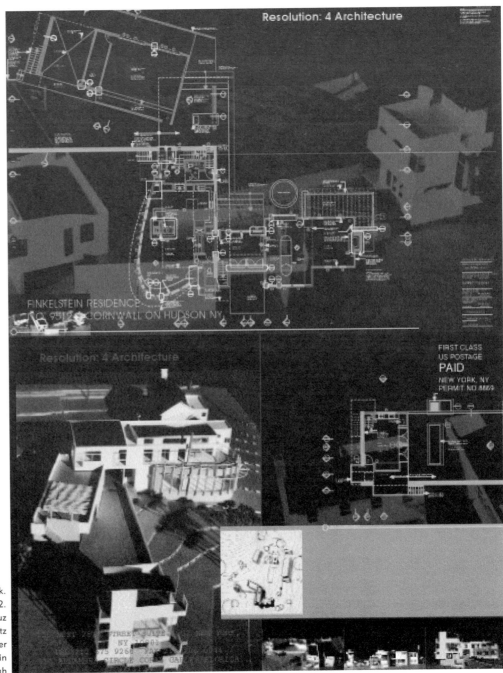

Finkelstein Residence, 9512 Cornwall on Hudson, New York.
See Color Plate 52.
Project architect: John DaCruz
Principals: Joseph Tanney, Robert Luntz
Project team: Heather Roberge, Clay Collier, Eric Liftin, Setu Shah, Jennifer
Pereira, Mario Gentile, Jeffrey Dvi-Vardhana, Kevin Bergin
Postcard: Setu Shah

Resolution: 4 Architecture

New York, New York

Freimark Residence, North Caldwell, New Jersey

Explanation of the Drawing Process and Technique

The three-dimensional drawing was created and rendered in Form-Z from a two-dimensional base drawing created in MiniCad.

Purpose of the Drawing

The computer model was created to study the relationship of the new volumes, rendered simply in red and green, with the existing roof system, which is rendered in gray. The existing volumes remain rendered as a wire frame. The composition was then used as a postcard intended for distribution to clients and colleagues.

Design Concept

The design of the Freimark residence consists of a series of volumes inserted into an existing roof composition, which weaves its way over existing volumes. The new volumes accommodate program while creating new interior spatial relationships.

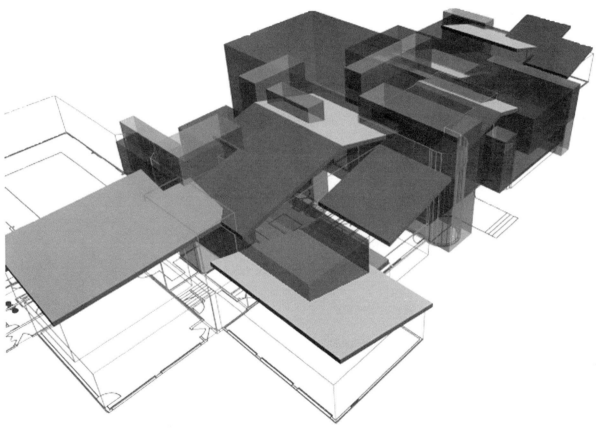

Freimark Residence, North Caldwell, New Jersey. See Color Plate 53.
Project architect: Erin Vali
Principals: Joseph Tanney, Robert Luntz
Project team: Jason Buchheit, Clay Collier, Setu Shah, Brian Bowman, Emanuel Stern, Ana Dobrovoljac, Mario Gentile
Postcard: Setu Shah

Christopher Rose

Rose Architecture, San Francisco, California

Porch Swing: A Pendulous Chair

Profile

Christopher Rose is a San Francisco-based architect and designer with a reputation for innovative and poetic spaces. His work is unique and contemporary, yet draws on a studied interpretation of history and local vernacular. In his projects, he responds to the rituals and dreams of a client and the actualities of place and program with a methodology that approaches design as a collaborative process. His firm, Rose Architecture, is known for its imaginative, site-specific, and informed design approach. The firm is often selected to work on projects that require creative and innovative thinking and has work ranging from houses and artist's spaces throughout the San Francisco Bay area, Rocky Mountain area, and rural Southern states to an EcoResort village in Cabo San Lucas, Mexico. Mr. Rose's projects and drawings have been published extensively and have been the focus of numerous design awards. The aim of his work is lightness, simplicity, and precision, and a spiritual celebration of everyday life.

Explanation of the Drawing Process and Technique

Rendered front elevation, plan, and side sectional elevations showing the movement of the swing. Pencil, Prismacolor pencil, graphite, India ink, and silver and gold metallic paint on Arches watercolor hotpress paper, 20"×30". The drawing is composed to convey the essence of movement embodied in the swing and the sculptural qualities and materials of the piece.

Purpose of the Drawing

The drawing serves as an interpretive model and assembly study for the furniture piece, and conveys the level of detail and combination of a variety of materials and configurations. It also serves to explain the path of movement of the swing relative to the floor.

Design Concept

Based on the movement of a pendulous gravity clock, like that in the Smithsonian Institution, the swing is designed as a suspended sculptural art element that animates the space it occupies by its movement and sweeping action across the floor. Due to its composition of metal, wood, and aluminum, its weight creates a very slow and deliberate movement through space and a pleasant ride for the user.

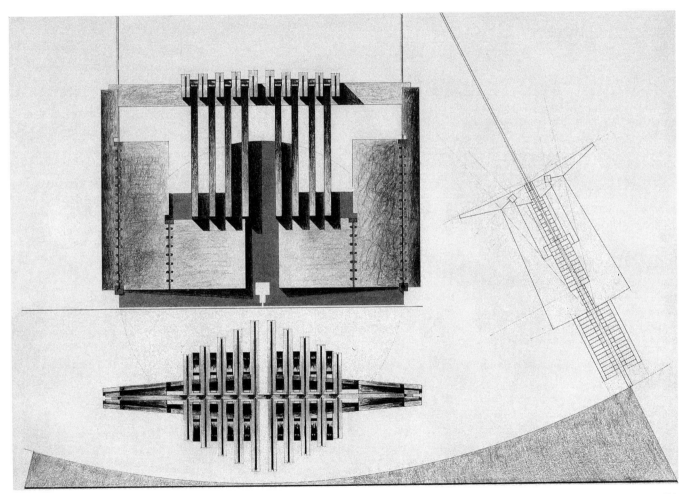

Porch Swing: A Pendulous Chair. See Color Plate 54.
Drawing: Christopher Rose

Schwartz Architects

New York, New York

New York Newsstand, New York, New York

Profile

Schwartz Architects is located in the Soho district of Manhattan. Frederic Schwartz was a recipient of the prestigious Rome Prize in Architecture in 1984–1985 and a National Endowment for the Arts Design Fellowship in 1982. Mr. Schwartz has won a number of major design competitions, including the new $81 million, 200,000-square-foot Staten Island Ferry Terminal at the tip of Manhattan (competition design with VSBA), the new $80 million, 350,000-square-foot Southwest Regional Capitol of France in Toulouse (joint venture with VSBA now under construction), and the East End Repertory Theater in Amagansett, New York. Mr. Schwartz was a 1973 Phi Beta Kappa graduate of the University of California at Berkeley and received a Master of Architecture from Harvard University in 1978. Mr. Schwartz has taught architectural design at Princeton University, Columbia University, Harvard University, Yale University, and the universities of Miami, North Carolina, Pennsylvania, and Milan. He has lectured on his work throughout America and Europe. He has also designed a number of award-winning houses and his work has been shown in various national and international exhibitions. Mr. Schwartz is also the author of three books: *Mother's House*, published by Rizzoli (in English, Japanese, and German); *Alan Buchsbaum: the Mechanics of Taste*, published by Monacelli Press; and *Venturi, Scott Brown and Associates*, published by Zanichelli (in Italian, English, Spanish, and German). He was formerly the director of the New York office of Venturi, Scott Brown and Associates (VSBA).

Explanation of the Drawing Process and Technique

The simplicity of the idea and the final development of the concept are illustrated by superimposing an enlarged bold freehand napkin sketch on a hand-tinted super-realistic photo collage. The collage was created by hand-cutting a black-and-white model photo on a street-corner shot of the newsstand's future location. Both photos were shot from the same angle with similar lighting. The collage was then re-shot and touched up digitally using Photoshop. Photoshop was also used to combine the black-and-white photos of the night and day views of the model with the collage and the superimposed sketch in fuchsia.

Purpose of the Drawing

The purpose of the drawing was to simultaneously illustrate both the "big idea," through the bold napkin sketch, and the "final results," as seen in a super-realistic collage, to the owner and city agencies.

Design Concept

The design was commissioned by the owner of an expanding chain of neighborhood restaurants in New York who sought to enrich the spirit and vitality of the city's sidewalk street life outside his locations. The elements of the design for the newsstand (winner of a 1996 NYC/AIA Design Award) are based on an abstraction of a printing press. The form and profile are bold and simple. The back and roof are a continuous "newspaper" skin of graffiti-resistant porcelain aluminum. The newspaper skin runs over a brushed stainless steel "press roller" that houses a pull-down security gate. The newsstand features a large, convenient printer's "drawer" that maximizes display and increases storage. The newsstand must look equally good open and closed. The drawer is supported on casters that roll on tracks in the floor, offering easy pull-out in the morning and quick push-in when closing at night. The "Big Apple red" drawer includes space for the display and storage of newspapers, magazines, and candy. The sides are green porcelain metal panels fastened to a steel frame with carriage bolts. The newsstand sits on a slab-heated concrete base for winter warmth. The newsstand as "news sculpture" offers an expressive and functional form that finds its place among the sidewalk iconography of fire hydrants, streetlights, and parking meters. Inexpensive and easy to fabricate, the newsstand conforms to the guidelines established by the New York City Department of Planning.

New York Newsstand, New York, New York. See Color Plate 55.
Design and drawing: Schwartz Architects

Jeffrey L. Sheppard of Roth + Sheppard Architects

Denver, Colorado

"Spyderco" Specialty Knife Manufacturers Headquarters, Golden, Colorado

Profile

Roth Sheppard Architects was established in 1983 as a four-person firm. Currently a studio of 10, the firm specializes in the creation of architecture that is derived from context, place, diagram, program, and systems. The balancing and juxtaposition of these concerns leads to the emotional strength and success of each project. The firm is nationally recognized for its expertise in police and municipal facility programming and design, with active projects in Hawaii, Washington, California, and Colorado. Other project types include restaurants and residential and educational facilities. Over the past 10 years, the firm has received six design awards from the AIA, and its design principal, Jeffrey L. Sheppard, was recognized as the 1989 Denver AIA Young Architect of the Year. Several of Mr. Sheppard's drawings have been acquired by the Denver Art Museum Department of Design and Architecture for its permanent collection.

Explanation of the Drawing Process and Technique

An underlying orthogonal grid system is used to organize the plan, the plan projected perspective, and the various elevations. Prismacolor, pencil, and charcoal media are used to create an angular and sharp-edged composition that communicates the metaphorical "knife" parti. Images are layered and composed such that lines and negative space from one image inform and influence the superimposed image from another, creating a "discovered" third image. Additionally, several scale variations of the same image are employed to stimulate the subconscious and create a drawing of greater depth and detail. The final image combines several media to further enhance the layered characteristic of the composition.

Purpose of the Drawing

As described above, the layering process leads to a "third" image that is derived from the superimposition of several related drawings. Within this "discovered" third image, we can begin to see relationships that coexist in plan, elevation, section, and perspective. This type of drawing allows us to explore these relationships and evaluate the subliminal connections that can successfully occur, creating a richer architectural experience. In this particular project, the knife metaphor and related terminology form the basis for the composition, alluding to the physical properties of edge, sharpness, angularity, and slicing.

Design Concept

This two-story building is located in a light industrial area bounded by nondescript storage and manufacturing facilities on all four sides. The building contains a mixture of office, manufacturing, and retailing functions related to the production of speciality knives. Planning, organization, and massing concepts explore the physical and metaphorical connection to the product being manufactured by exploring the notion of sharpness, angularity, sectional slicing, and edge.

"Spyderco" Specialty Knife Manufacturers Headquarters,
Golden, Colorado.
Design: Roth + Sheppard Architects
Drawing: Jeffrey L. Sheppard

S P Y D E R C O

Jeffrey L. Sheppard of Roth + Sheppard Architects

Denver, Colorado

Colorado House, S.W. Colorado Border

Explanation of the Drawing Process and Technique

The first board of a two-board composition using a collage of media including Prisma-color, charcoal, graphite, pen and ink, and wax-based crayon on 1000H paper. Approximately 16 different scaled images are overlaid to reinforce the design parti, 24"×36".

Purpose of the Drawing

This drawing is an expression of the emotion of the parti, derived from the layered impact of the tectonic image. Completed during the schematic design phase of the project, this drawing uses an underlying orthogonal grid system to organize plan, section, and elevation into a composition of layered two-dimensional scaled images. Although it is possible to read the individual characteristics of each scaled image, the layering of the drawings is intended to communicate the emotional and physical power of the agrarian context, landscape forms, and spatial experiences. Images are layered and composed such that lines and negative space from one inform and influence the superimposed image from another, creating a "discovered" third image. Within this "discovered" third image, we can begin to see relationships that coexist in plan, elevation, and section.

Design Concept

The juxtaposition of the mountains and plains forms the site of this winning entry in a regional design competition titled "9 Houses." Agrarian imagery in both plan and section provides the patterns from which the design has evolved. Gridded and eroded landscape, container elements, water towers, and irrigated landscape are physically and metaphorically explored to formulate a variety of spatial, processional, and enclosure experiences for the functional program of the house. Note how the four-square plan is explored in section, elevation, and the center of the floor plan.

Colorado House, S.W. Colorado Border.
Design: Roth + Sheppard Architects
Drawing: Jeffrey L. Sheppard

Ashton Smith

New Orleans, Louisiana

City Hall Proposal, Eunice, Louisiana

Profile

Ashton Smith is a practicing architect, developing architectural projects with individual qualities and characters. He also works in the professional theater as a scenic and lighting designer, and currently teaches at Southern University School of Architecture in Baton Rouge, Louisiana.

Explanation of the Drawing Process and Technique

Photography, hand rendering, and collage. First, the site was photographed and the design proposal was hand-rendered on to the photograph. The adjacent neighborhood was photographed and neighborhood images were then mounted on to the rendering in areas where the glass becomes reflective. The completed presentation image is 30"×70".

Purpose of the Drawing

This presentation technique was considered the best communicative tool for a "modern" proposal to be presented to the town council of a small Southern community that considered modern architecture radical. The circumstance demanded a realistic image of the proposal.

Design Concept

A true 1960s concept: a "Miesian" invisible solution that responds to the community needs and relates contextually because of its reflecting images of the community (storage barns, grain silos, and turn-of-the-century public buildings).

PROPOSED CITY HALL AND JAIL
eunice, louisiana

E GUILLET   CITY CLERK & TAX COLLECTOR
M DAIGLE   CHIEF OF POLICE
LAS YOUNG   CITY JUDGE
LEY & CLAYTON   CITY ATTORNEY   DR. J. J. STAGG   MAYOR
DAVID DEVILLIER   ASSISTANT CITY ATTORNEY   J. DUDLEY GUILLORY   MAYOR PRO TEM
CE BELLOW   MARSHALL · WARD ONE   ASHTON SMITH · ARCHITECT · NOVEMBER 19

City Hall Proposal, Eunice, Louisiana.
Drawing: Ashton Smith

Ashton Smith with Dan Branch

New Orleans, Louisiana

Wales Opera House Competition, Wales, United Kingdom

Profile

Ashton Smith and Dan Branch are both practicing architects. Ashton Smith also works in the professional theater as a scenic and lighting designer, and currently teaches at Southern University School of Architecture in Baton Rouge, Louisiana. Dan Branch is currently teaching in the department of architecture, University of Southwestern Louisiana, Lafayette, Louisiana.

Explanation of the Drawing Process and Technique

Interior of a proposed opera house. Hand-rendered drawing on a high-contrast print of an interior study model. The model interior was photographed with an extremely high-contrast film to achieve a rendering-like effect. After inserting the people, furniture, light fixtures, and so on, a color photograph of an actual opera stage production (including the orchestra in the pit) was mounted onto the rendering. Final size is 24"×36".

Purpose of the Drawing

For the purpose of studying site lines and acoustics, interior study models were constructed. The final interior design was then photographed. The designers felt this would best describe their competition entry proposal.

Design Concept

The concept of the opera house interior was a response to the question of which configuration best offered quality performance, both acoustically and visually. This was explored through the use of large-scale study models in order to establish good sight lines within a good acoustical environment.

Wales Opera House Competition, Wales, United Kingdom. See Color Plate 56.
Design: Ashton Smith and Dan Branch
Drawing: Ashton Smith

Smith-Miller + Hawkinson Architects

New York, New York

Shilla Daechi Building (as Shown at the Venice Bienniale, 1996)

Profile

Smith-Miller + Hawkinson Architects, founded in 1983, is an architectural firm in New York, consisting of two principals, Henry Smith-Miller and Laurie Hawkinson, and 12 employees. Smith-Miller + Hawkinson's projects span a wide scope, from small to very large and complex interiors, from building additions to freestanding single or multiuse buildings. Recent projects include a new mixed-use building for Samsung in Seoul, Korea; the North Carolina Museum of Art "master" site plan and project (which opened in April 1997) for an outdoor cinema and amphitheater, with artist Barbara Kruger and landscape architect Nicholas Quennell; the Wall Street Ferry Terminal for Pier 11 in Lower Manhattan; design guidelines for the Battery Park City Authority of New York's Hudson River Ferry Terminal; and the Corning Glass Center 2000 Project, a three-phase, $60 million millennium project, currently under construction. Smith-Miller + Hawkinson was one of six American architectural firms invited to exhibit in the Italian Pavilion at the 1996 Venice Bienniale for Architecture, and one of four firms participating in the Fabrications installation at the Museum of Modern Art in New York. *Smith-Miller + Hawkinson*, a monograph, was published in 1995 by Gustavo Gili Editoriale. The firm is also included in the film "The New Modernists" by Michael Blackwood. Smith-Miller + Hawkinson stresses strong interests in a general culture of architecture: its design and technological histories, as well as its complex and changing relationship to society. Of these changes, the firm is particularly interested in focusing on the ways in which the architectural program—the location and accommodation of functions, activities, and services—can be developed through innovative interpretations that are sensitive to and transformative of contemporary cultural needs and ideas.

Explanation of the Drawing Process and Technique

Photo collage and digital compositing.

Purpose of the Drawing

This collage drawing is one of 27 panels that were printed on a large-format ink-jet plotter to the dimension of 3'×3', mounted on foam core and assembled into a 9'×27'-long exhibition as one of 6 architectural firms representing the United States in the Italian Pavilion exhibition, "Emerging Voices," at the 1996 Architecture Bienniale in Venice.

Design Concept

The drawings are intended to provide a view into two projects simultaneously (the Shilla Daechi Building in Seoul, Korea, and the amphitheater and outdoor cinema for the North Carolina Museum of Art) by providing drawings and images at a series of scales, so that the panel may be read up close or from very far (a large image about 9'×9' was best read from across the room, while the smallest images of 2"×3" might be read only from a short distance). In addition, "footnotes" of other projects and related images are assembled in a kind of water line at eye level, for reference, along the entire 27-foot length.

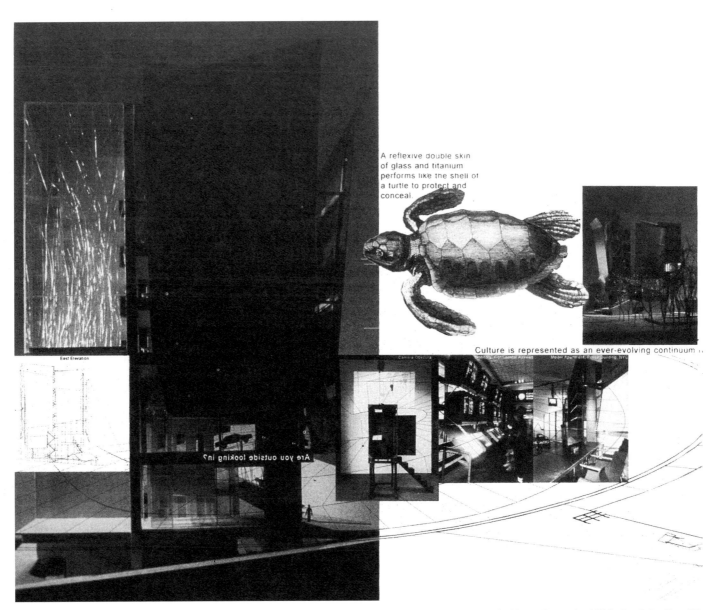

A reflexive double skin
of glass and titanium
performs like the shell of
a turtle to protect and
conceal.

Culture is represented as an ever-evolving continuum

Shilla Daechi Building (as shown at the Venice Bienniale, 1996). See Color Plate 57.
Design and drawing: Smith-Miller + Hawkinson Architects

Smith-Miller + Hawkinson Architects

New York, New York

Corning Glass Center 2000

Explanation of the Drawing Process and Technique

This drawing was made using Softimage™ three-dimensional animation software by importing design development drawings, creating an arrival sequence, and selecting the still from the resulting animation.

Purpose of the Drawing

The drawing was produced for the client to provide an "image" of the building to the community and the corporation.

Design Concept

The drawing shows the glass entry of the new Visitors Center building, and the jitney (the transportation link) as a red blur at the left of the drawing.

Corning Glass Center 2000. See Color Plate 58.
Design and drawing: Smith-Miller + Hawkinson Architects

Thomas Sofranko

Assistant Professor, School of Architecture, Louisiana State University, Baton Rouge, Louisiana

Spirit House 5

Profile

Thomas Sofranko is a 1991 graduate of Kent State University School of Architecture. He is currently an assistant professor of architecture at Louisiana State University, primarily teaching design studios and various critical seminars. He is also a design consultant in the office of Julian Thaddeus White, AIA. Most recently, the office has been involved with medical and religious structures.

Explanation of the Drawing Process and Technique

Ink on vellum, film, and photographs. The extreme site for this project also serves as a critical focus for the drawing. By diagonally mirro ring the site section about the section cut line of the plan, the drawing establishes the site/section relationship as a representational device that graphically reinforces the design concept. The photographs provide base and contrast, as well as initializing the differentiation of layers.

Purpose of the Drawing

This drawing is one of a series of drawings for a design investigation which, in turn, is one in a series of seven "Spirit Houses." The Spirit Houses are an ongoing series that investigates various ideas of order, entrenchment, and domesticity. This drawing was specifically produced for an international traveling exhibition.

Design Concept

The Spirit Houses are concerned with structuring the simultaneous conditions of emptiness and immensity—awkwardness of form, obfuscation of scale, and dissolution of contextual reference—to render man insignificant. In assigning man this reduced role, the work seeks to give the made privilege over the maker. In doing so, we are included as part of nature, rather than outside of it; we are not the constructors of myths, we are a part of them. This condition is also characteristic of the work of Ledoux, Boulee, and de Chirico—a melancholic void waits to be filled with a human element.

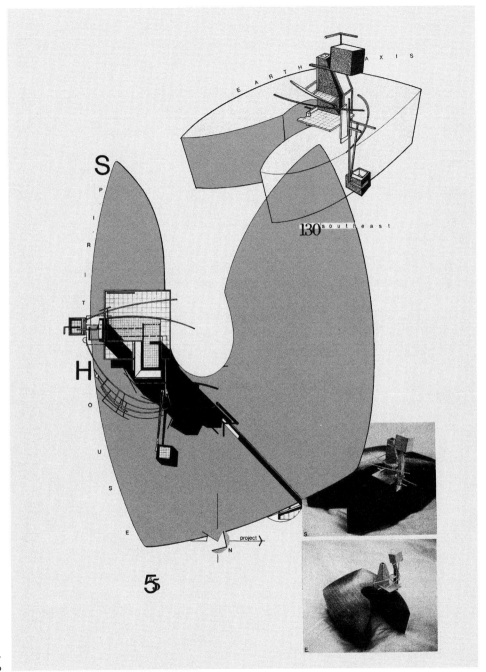

Spirit House 5. See Color Plate 59.
Design and drawing: Thomas Sofranko

Shin Takamatsu

Shin Takamatsu Architects & Associates, Kyoto, Japan

Gotsu Community Center, Gotsu-shi, Japan

Profile

Internationally recognized Japanese architect Shin Takamatsu first attracted attention after completing a series of buildings dotted around the former Japanese capital of Kyoto. Designed fortress-like to withstand the rigors of the modern city, they are produced apparently by means of a "super technology." These buildings display technology-crafted finishes and signify the machine metaphor of metal joinery. Mr. Takamatsu's recent works are in large scale with complex functions. Shin Takamatsu has a reputation for being innovative, unique, and contemporary, reflecting an interpretation of technology and related imagery. In addition to his professional practice, Mr. Takamatsu is a professor of architecture at Kyoto University.

Explanation of the Drawing Process and Technique

Shadowed plan with site context. Pencil on Kent paper (790 mm × 1090 mm).

Purpose of the Drawing

Presentation drawing showing both interior and exterior spaces in one drawing.

Design Concept

This is a 700-seat multipurpose hall, a composite architecture consisting of a library containing 70,000 books and local reference materials, offices for city social welfare activities, and a plaza and recreational space for city residents. A wooded area, 30 meters in width and 170 meters in length, has been a buffer, but at the same time carries out the function of environmentally dissolving the boundary between the two zones. Incidentally, architecture in this case functions as one kind of wall: a huge wall, possessing a silhouette, that is born from the accurate transference of the functional arrangement from the plan's program. At the southeastern boundary, this wall is loaded with an installed device of winking constellations in a clear and simple stratified construction. To intensely present the direction of movement for a variety of activities through this stratified space, depending on how one views the situation, such a space could be seen as very inconvenient. On many levels, the workability of this architecture depends on whether or not the strength can be developed to control such inconvenience.

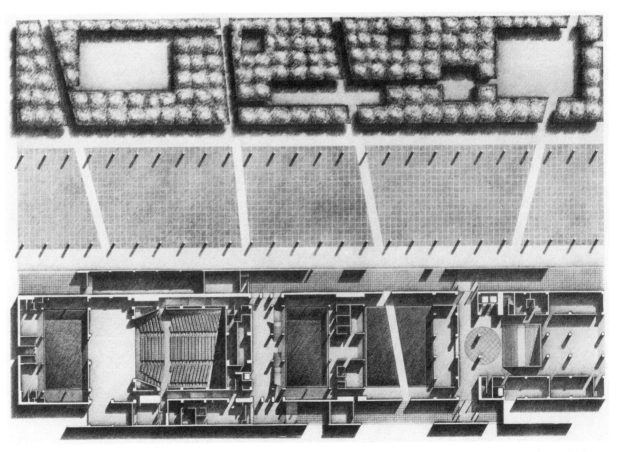

Gotsu Community Center, Gotsu-shi, Japan.
Design and drawing: Shin Takamatsu Architects & Associates

Shin Takamatsu

Shin Takamatsu Architects & Associates, Kyoto, Japan

Kunibiki Messe, Matsue, Japan

Explanation of the Drawing Process and Technique

Acrylic color applied with an airbrush on white heavyweight tracing paper.

Purpose of the Drawing

Presentation drawing illustrating the night environment, highlighting relationships of glazed and opaque surfaces.

Design Concept

This 16,000-square-meter building accommodates an international trade fair center and congress hall and offices. The local myth of how the country was created was visualized in the composition of the "Communication Salon" located in the center of the building. The system is formed on the line drawn between two elements. By distorting this line, the design tries to realize the space that contains all the elements inside.

Kunibiki Messe, Matsue, Japan. See Color Plate 60.
Design and drawing: Shin Takamatsu Architects & Associates

Christine L. Tedesco

Principal, RSCT Architecture + Design, Pendleton, South Carolina

"Aqueducts, Cisterns and the Tarantella," No. 1/Aggregate

Profile

Christine L. Tedesco is a designer and, with her husband, principal of RSCT Architecture + Design in Pendleton, South Carolina. The practice consists of the design and production of a variety of work, including architecture, products, furniture, lighting, graphics, textiles, and photography. This project was conducted by Ms. Tedesco during an 18-month period while serving as adjunct resident professor at the Charles E. Daniel Center for Building Research and Urban Study in Genoa, Italy. The project was supported in part by a grant from the South Carolina Arts Commission. The study began as an investigation into certain aspects of Italian society and culture. This initially led to consideration of the tarantella, a southern Italian folk dance for women, while conducting a parallel survey of the medieval aqueduct system in the city of Genoa, Italy.

Explanation of the Drawing Process and Technique

Composite drawing No. 1/aggregate information, ink on multiple layers of double-matted Mylar, 18"×24". Each side of the double-matted Mylar, as a potential drawing surface, gathers seemingly disparate information, allowing it to advance or recede depending on the reading and which surface contains the information. This method, although using conventional techniques, upsets the traditional viewpoint from which the reader receives the information, thus allowing for multiple readings, each of which will inform the next move.

Purpose of the Drawing

The purpose was to investigate the medieval aqueduct system in the city of Genoa, Italy, and also a southern Italian folk dance, the tarantella. Through overlays, the drawing explored various relationships between these two seemingly disparate topics.

Design Concept

This drawing marks the first in a series of generative hybrid drawings that attempts to transfer and transform the basic information gathered in the previous overlay drawing series. This composite contains selected elements drawn from the entire set of basic information. A tarantula spider (from which the tarantella gets its name) section is layered under this grouping.

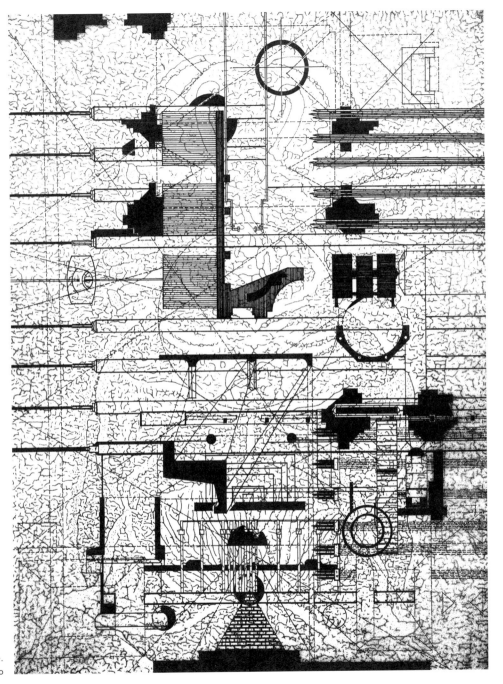

"Aqueducts, Cisterns and the Tarantella," No. 1/aggregate.
Drawing: Christine L. Tedesco

Principal, RSCT Architecture + Design, Pendleton, South Carolina

"Aqueducts, Cisterns and the Tarantella," No. 3/Aggregate

Explanation of the Drawing Process and Technique

Composite drawing No. 3/aggregate information, sepia Mylar, 18"×24". This drawing represents a reassemblage of previously recorded information selected intuitively. Images include a plan view of a Baroque church, which sets the stage for the tarantella, and orthographic views of the aqueduct and pipe systems.

Purpose of the Drawing

The purpose was to investigate the medieval aqueduct system in the city of Genoa, Italy, and also a southern Italian folk dance, the tarantella. Through overlays, the drawing explored various relationships between these two seemingly disparate topics.

Design Concept

Using a vacuum frame and photo reproductive techniques, various layers of information are taken from the previous set of drawings. Several of these composites are produced with increasing complexity and intensity. Conventional readings and meanings are subverted, allowing new information and interpretations to emerge. With each new composite drawing, orthographically projected conventions from the previous overlay series simultaneously intensify and fragment, clarifying certain elements while obscuring others. This deliberately causes a rereading or misreading of the image, as the familiar is obscured.

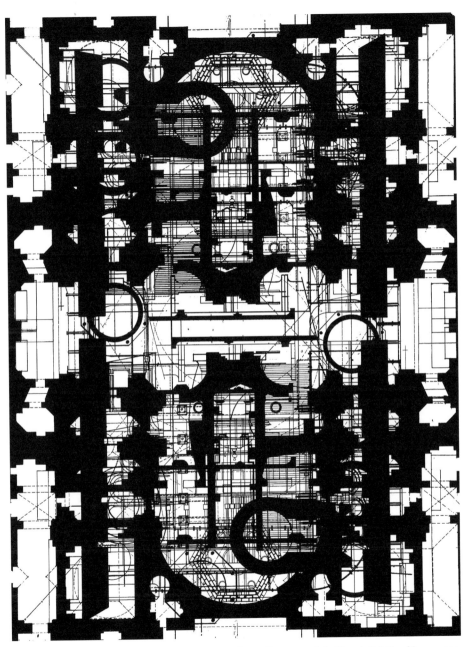

"Aqueducts, Cisterns and the Tarantella" No. 3/aggregate.
Drawing: Christine L. Tedesco

Bernard Tschumi Architects

New York/Paris

In Between, Le Fresnoy National Studio for Contemporary Arts, Tourcoing, France

Profile

Internationally acclaimed architect Bernard Tschumi studied architecture in his native Switzerland, and subsequently started teaching at London's Architectural Association. He founded Bernard Tschumi Architects in 1987, with offices in New York and Paris. He has held professorship and administrative positions at various architectural schools, including Princeton University, New York's Cooper Union School of Architecture, and Yale University, and currently is the dean of the Graduate School of Architecture, Planning, and Preservation at Columbia University in New York. Among many award-winning projects, his most famous realized works are the Follies in the Parc de la Villette, Paris, and the Glass Video Gallery in Groningen, the Netherlands.

Explanation of the Drawing Process and Technique

Plan; computer-generated night simulation.

Purpose of the Drawing

Presentation drawing showing intensity of night illumination.

Design Concept

Eight thousand square meters of an international center for the contemporary arts (a school, a film studio, a *mediatheque*, spectacle and exhibition halls, two cinemas, laboratories for research and production, administrative offices, housing, and a bar/restaurant) inserted into the existing Le Fresnoy, built in the 1920s. Conceptually, the project was interpreted as a succession of boxes inside a box. Under the large electronic roof are the boxes of the existing building, most hereafter sheltered from the bad weather. The new facilities located in the existing volumes were conceived as technically autonomous boxes while maintaining the fluidity of the Fresnoy spaces. At Le Fresnoy, the design intent speaks of an "architecture-event" rather than an "architecture-object." The interstitial space between the new and old roofs becomes a place of fantasies and experiments (filming and other exploratory works on space and time). The space in between becomes a condenser of interdisciplinary investigations between teaching and research, art and cinema, music and image.

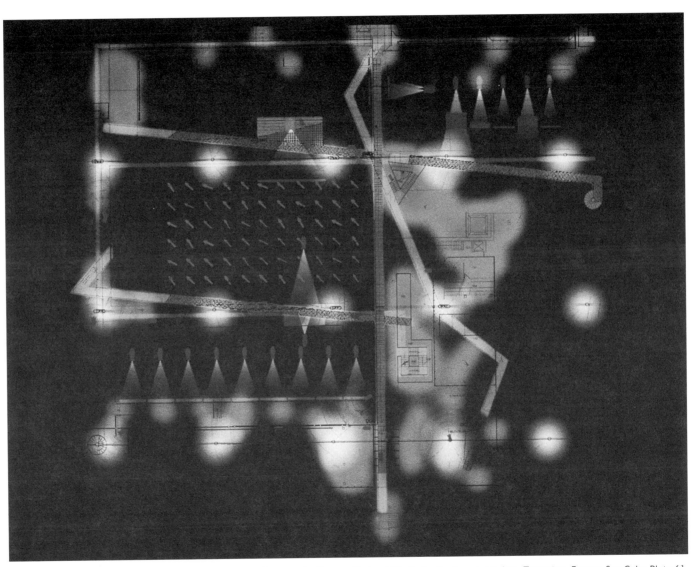

In Between, Le Fresnoy National Studio for Contemporary Arts, Tourcoing, France. See Color Plate 61.
Design and drawing: Bernard Tschumi Architects

M. Saleh Uddin

Professor, School of Architecture, Southern University, Baton Rouge, Louisiana

Grid Clock

Profile

M. Saleh Uddin is currently a professor and associate dean at the Southern University School of Architecture in Baton Rouge, Louisiana. In a teaching career spanning 18 years, he has taught students at Kent State University, Savannah College of Art and Design, and Bangladesh University of Engineering and Technology in Dhaka. He has won numerous awards for his design and rendering work, including the American Society of Architectural Perspectivists Juror's Award of Excellence. Professor Uddin, author of this book, has published and presented papers at national and international conferences, and is the author of *Composite Drawing: Techniques for Architectural Design Presentation* and *Axonometric and Oblique Drawing: A 3D Construction, Rendering and Design Guide*, both published by McGraw-Hill.

Explanation of the Drawing Process and Technique

A three-dimensional computer model was created first, using Form·Z Renderzone. A life-size scale model in basswood, mount board, and paint was then constructed, using the computer model as a guide. This final image is a digital manipulation of both computer and hand models integrated as one image file. The bottom left-hand image is the photograph of the built model scanned into the digital file, where the other Form·Z models were imported.

Purpose of the Drawing

Comparing the computer model with the actual completed hand model of the clock design was the primary intention of this hybrid image. Documentation as a digital file, as well as in hard copy printout, was the end product of this image.

Design Concept

The perception and dimension of "time" have always remained an abstract entity to us. Visual images are required to transform the perception of time. As a measured unit, the concept of 60 seconds in a minute, and 60 minutes in an hour is becoming questionable as we move into the digital environment. For example, a microwave oven has to read both 100 and 60 units as one minute. The emotional perception of time scale is also significantly associated with environmental conditions, such as light, acoustics, and quality of space around us. Revisualizing the time scale was a concern of this project.

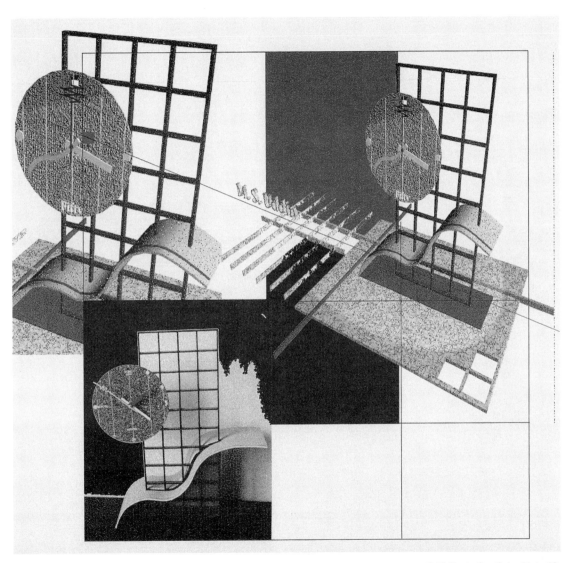

Grid Clock. See Color Plate 62.
Design and drawing: M. Saleh Uddin

Professor, School of Architecture, Southern University, Baton Rouge, Louisiana

Rahman Residence, Dhaka, Bangladesh

Explanation of the Drawing Process and Technique

Photocollage using presentation plans, Form·Z model, AutoCAD three-dimensional drawing, construction plans, and photographs of the completed front facade and interior stair details. Photographs superimposed on drawings copied on color Pantone film and negative prints. Final size 24"×36".

Purpose of the Drawing

The purpose of this image was to document graphically the process of the design, from study drawings to construction drawings and, finally, completed exterior and interior. This image (now in the client's collection) constantly reminds the owner of his involvement with the design of the building at various stages of its execution.

Design Concept

One-family residence with the provision for vertical expansion without sacrificing the privacy of the current design. Restricted site boundaries forced the design to be sculpted from a cubic mass volume. Subtracted mass in the front protects the glazed wall and sucks air inside the building, which counterbalances the double-height void in the dining area, facilitating natural airflow year-round. All openings were carefully designed (most openings pushed inward to avoid direct confrontation with climatic extremes) to respond to the environmental conditions of the region's hot, humid climate.

Rahman Residence, Dhaka, Bangladesh. See Color Plate 63.
Design and drawing: M. Saleh Uddin

Mehrdad Yazdani

Design Principal, Dworsky Associates, Los Angeles, California

Overland House, Los Angeles, California

Profile

Mehrdad Yazdani joined Dworsky Associates in 1994 as a design principal, and was subsequently named director of design. He brings to his projects more than a decade of innovative architectural design experience. His philosophy of design is based on maintaining an environment of exploration in the design studio, tempered with a realistic sense of each client's needs and the importance of the pragmatic details. Mr. Yazdani's work has been featured in both national and international publications, such as *A+U*, *The Los Angeles Times*, *Progressive Architecture*, *Architectural Record*, *L'ARCA*, *Architectural Design*, *GA Houses*, and *Architecture*, and has been exhibited in major museums and galleries in San Francisco, Los Angeles, Boston, and New York. His work is currently part of the permanent collections of both the New York and San Francisco Museums of Modern Art. He has judged various American Institute of Architecture Awards competitions and has lectured at a number of architectural institutions.

Explanation of the Drawing Process and Technique

Composite photomontage combining model photograph and floor plan. Black-and-white model photograph superimposed on reverse (negative) ink-drawn floor plan. A black-and-white model photograph was photocopied in a copy machine to eliminate middle tones in the photograph and to highlight the features of the building forms. The reversed floor plan was then combined with the photograph for the final effect.

Purpose of the Drawing

The drawing was composed for the purpose of presentation, as well as for publication and documentation.

Design Concept

The house attempts to address what is primary to the fields of both architecture and fashion design, the human figure, and to explore the commonality that is found in both. As in fashion design, the generation of this project takes its initial cues from how the human figure is affected by its primary environment. This methodology then becomes an active process, similar to those found in painting and sculpture, using the sensual human shape and superimposing patterns, cutting, assimilating, and rearranging—in a sense, collaging. In the end, it produces a new geometry, which seeks to create a new perception of volumes and spaces.

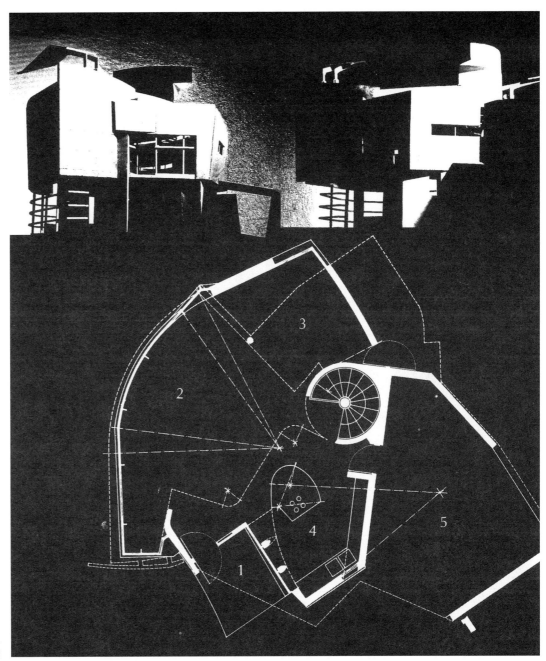

Overland House, Los Angeles, California.
Design and drawing: Mehrdad Yazdani

Art Zendarski for Dworsky Associates, Los Angeles

Zendarski Studio, San Francisco, California

Federal Building and United States Courthouse, Las Vegas, Nevada

Profile

Zendarski Studio provides presentation services for architects and developers nationwide. The office meets clients' objectives while drawing from a wealth of experience in a variety of techniques, including computer graphics and other traditional media: pencil, watercolor, pen & ink, oil & acrylic.

Explanation of the Drawing Process and Technique

Black pencil on paper, 20"×23". The bold geometry of the building shapes and bright Las Vegas sunlight set the stage for the choice of media. Rendering in black pencil provided the means both to express the architectural elements under the entry canopy in fine detail and to capture the overall formal character of the design. Computer drawings provided a thorough study analysis for view selection. The perspective layout and shadow studies were also accurately generated by computer. The drawing was then hand-rendered in black pencil.

Purpose of the Drawing

The main purpose of the rendering was to communicate a complex building design to distinguished clients in a clear and precise manner. Second, the drawing was to aid in the internal approval process. The rendering also provided the architectural firm with a valuable promotional tool.

Design Concept

In addition to being a symbol of federal presence in the city, this courthouse will also be responsive to the surrounding city and environmental concerns and establish a design precedent for large-scale public buildings. The building is situated on the southern end of Las Vegas Boulevard, acting as a symbolic cornerstone for the edge of downtown. The project opens up to embrace the city and protects the entry plaza from prevailing winds and the southern sun. The "L" configuration creates a diagonal axis, relating its public face to downtown and the existing courthouse, which is adjacent to the new project. The processional entry sequence filters movement from the city to the raised plaza along a reflecting pool, into the urban scaled space under the canopy, through the security checkpoint, and into the light-filled public lobby. The syntax of the internal organization is largely driven by the relationships among public, secure, and restricted spaces.

Federal Building and United States Courthouse, Las Vegas, Nevada.
Design: Dworsky Associates, Los Angeles, California
Drawing: Art Zendarski

LSU Lecture Poster. See Color Plate 64.
Courtesy: Form:uLA/Bryan Cantley + Kevin O'Donnell

Hybrid Drawing Techniques by Contemporary Architects and Designers